SPECIFIC PRAYER

How To Pray What You Need To Pray To See Answers To Your Prayers

DR. SHELDON D. NEWTON

All Rights Reserved ©

Unless otherwise indicated, all Scripture quotations are taken from the King James Version of the Holy Bible.

Scripture quotations marked AMP are from The Amplified Bible, Old Testament copyright ©1965, 1987 by the Zondervan Corporation. The Amplified New Testament copyright 1954, 1958, 1987 by the Lockman Foundation. Used by permission.

Scriptures taken from The Message Bible, copyright © 1993, 1994, 1995, 1996, 2000, 2001, 2002. Used by permission of NavPress Publishing Group.

Specific Kinds Of Prayer
Copyright © 2020 Sheldon D. Newton
All Rights Reserved

Cover Design by GLA Studios

Edited by Deborah Moore of Moore Editing Services

Sheldon D. Newton
P. O. Box N-10257
Nassau, Bahamas
Email the Author: sheldond.newton@gmail.com
A JCCMI Production

ACKNOWLEDGMENT

God always has people who help you accomplish what He has called you to do. And when it comes to writing and publishing books He places upon my heart, it is no different.

I would like to acknowledge Minister Deborah Moore of Moore Editing Services who helped with the editing of the manuscript; and to GLA Graphics, the designer of such a beautiful cover. These people are the ones who helped to make it happen. May God bless and favor each of you for the kindness and assistance you continually give me. Together we are influencing the world for God.

DEDICATION

I dedicate this book to all who are hungry to know God in a real, personal and intimate way. If you are hungry for more of His Presence in your life, this one is for you!

Dr. Sheldon D. Newton

CONTENTS

Acknowledgment

Dedication

Preface

Chapter One: What Is Prayer......................11

Chapter Two: Why Pray..........................19

Chapter Three: What To Pray For...............23

Chapter Four: How To Pray Specifically.......37

Chapter Five: Assured Of An Answer...........55

Chapter Six: Have Faith In God.................75

Chapter Seven: Giving God Glory 85

Chapter Eight: Faith & Patience.................107

Chapter Nine: Obstacle Of Un-forgiveness.....113

Chapter Ten: Praying For The Lost..............127

Chapter Eleven: Praying In The Spirit 133

Chapter Twelve: In The Spirit For Others.......149

Chapter Thirteen: Developing A Prayer Life...157

Specific Kinds Of Prayer

FOREWORD

In a world of unprecedented upheaval in every area of life, people are crying out for answers to the madness! Christians and non-Christians alike are being shaken to their very core.

The head of the church - Jesus Christ - is once again saying to the church, ***"My house shall be called the house of prayer!"*** In this book **"Praying for Results"** Bishop Newton gives us the answer for being able to gain peace, comfort, joy – answers we are looking for, and great victory in the midst of all the chaos!!!

He teaches practical truths on prayer and its absolute essential importance and privilege for every born again child of God. At the center of every great relationship is great communication. The truths taught in this book, when applied consistently in your life, will absolutely revolutionize your prayer life – your communion with your Father, the Creator of the universe!

Jesus gave His life to make the same incredible fellowship He enjoyed with His Father a reality in the life of every man, woman, boy and girl who accept His sacrifice and become a part of God's family - and if you are born again, that includes you!!!

As you read this book, prepare to embark on a journey into the sweetest fellowship known to man - communion with your Father!!

Deborah Moore
Minister & Author
One Thing Is Needful

PREFACE

This guide and manual on building and developing an effective prayer life is written in a practical manner that the reader may be able to apply himself or herself immediately.

Prayer is the process through which we draw nearer to the Heart of the Father on an on-going basis, experiencing His Presence and knowing His reality, through the releasing of His power on humanity's behalf. God is still a prayer answering, covenant-keeping God. He has always answered the earnest, heart-felt prayer of His people and He always will.

There are some things which will never happen until we pray. There are people who stand in need of deliverance; stand in need of salvation; stand in need of healing or provision; stand in need of the Father's wisdom, help, comfort and strength. We may also stand in need of these things on a consistent basis. We need God. Prayer is how we approach Him and receive from Him. It is essential that we learn how to pray effectively and enjoy the wonders of answered prayer.

May this guide help you as you seek the Face of the Father and draw near to Him through prayer!

Specific Kinds Of Prayer

Chapter One
WHAT IS PRAYER

Prayer is essential to our walk with God!

However, many people have false views regarding prayer. They have been taught wrong. They have not been taught in line with God's Word. They may have received their views on prayer from their religious up-bringing. They may have received wrong views based upon their denominational training.

Prayer is not a religious thing. It is an actual avenue of communicating with the One true and Living God. He is a Person, a very real Person, and One Who we can fellowship with on a constant basis. Here are some facts about prayer, based on God's Word.

Prayer is talking with God

It is not just repeating words and phrases continually, hoping that one day God will hear and answer. It is actually talking things over with Him and being real with Him. God wants to hear our hearts.

Matthew 15:8
8 This people draweth nigh unto me with their mouth, and honoureth me with their lips; but their heart is far from me.

When we speak to God, it must be from the heart. He has promised that it is when we seek Him with all of our hearts that we shall find Him.

Jeremiah 29: 12-13
12 Then shall ye call upon me, and ye shall go and pray unto me, and I will hearken unto you.
13 And ye shall seek me, and find me, when ye shall search for me with all your heart.

So the first thing we must understand is that prayer is a heart thing. It is speaking to and communing with God from our hearts. Now what does this mean? First, it means that when we pray, we must be real with God. We must not tell Him words that we do not mean. We should not pray words just because they sound good and eloquent. **Our words need to have our hearts in them.** Our words must come from deep within. When we speak with the Lord, we need to ensure that what are praying and saying to Him is what we really mean. After all, we are speaking to God – to the Creator and Sustainer of heaven and earth. Speaking from our hearts in a humble manner shows that we reverence and respect Him for Who He is!

Second, it means that our prayers should always be prayed to God and never to impress people. Many pray what appears to be prayers in order for people to be impressed with how they pray. They love hearing people tell them how good they sound and how deep their prayer life is. They sound like the Pharisees Jesus referred to in the Book of Matthew.

Matthew 6:5
5 And when thou prayest, thou shalt not be as the hypocrites are: for they love to pray standing in the synagogues and in the corners of the streets, that they may be seen of men. Verily I say unto you, They have their reward.

The Message Translation of this verse really stands out. Listen to this:

Matthew 6:5 (MSG)
5 "And when you come before God, don't turn that into a theatrical production either. All these people making a regular show of their prayers, hoping for stardom! Do you think God sits in a box seat?"

If we truly desire for God to hear and answer our prayers, we cannot pray to impress people. Again, our heart must be in our prayers.

We must speak to God – not speak as though we are speaking to God, when in reality we are just speaking so that we can be praised by those listening to us. Whether we are praying privately or publicly, we must ensure that we center our attention and focus upon the Lord.

This is the essence of what real praying is about. We are communing and communicating with the Father God. We are seeking His Face. We are speaking with Him. He is God. He is a very real Person. He is the Most Intelligent Person in existence. And He longs for a close relationship with us.

When You Pray Say, "Our Father"

When the disciples of the Lord Jesus Christ asked Him to teach them to pray, He replied by saying the following words:

Matthew 6:9
9 After this manner therefore pray ye: Our Father which art in heaven, Hallowed be thy name.

Wonder of wonders, the Lord Jesus Christ said that when we address the Father, we are to call Him Father. What a glorious truth!

While Yahweh is God, we have the honor given to us by the Lord Himself to call God Father!

That very word describe a place of intimacy and acceptance that are thrilling, exciting and absolutely marvelous. God – the Creator and Sustainer of the universe – the Elohim – Jehovah – the Sovereign Lord – gives us the honor of calling Him Father. He has made us His very sons and daughters, through Christ Jesus. We are actually born of Him – Spirit to spirit. His Holy Spirit has recreated our spirits, making us new creations in Jesus Christ, children of the Living God.

John 1: 12-13
12 But as many as received him, to them gave he power to become the sons of God, even to them that believe on his name:
13 Which were born, not of blood, nor of the will of the flesh, nor of the will of man, but of God.

(Read also, John 3: 1-6 & 2Corinthians 5: 17-18.)

According to scripture, we are now able to call God Almighty, **ABBA**.

Romans 8: 15-16
15 For ye have not received the spirit of bondage again to fear; but ye have received the Spirit of adoption, whereby we cry, Abba, Father.
16 The Spirit itself beareth witness with our spirit, that we are the children of God:

This is a term of extremely close significance. It speaks of an actual relationship. We are not just children of God religiously. It is not just a cliché or something we say because it sounds good. In Jesus Christ and through His shed blood, we are actually children of God, born of God. We belong! We belong to Him.

In this standing, we can come boldly – without fear, shame or intimidation – into the very Presence of the

Living God and make our requests known. We have a standing invitation to do so. God wants us to. He loves our fellowship.

Hebrews 4:16
16 Let us therefore come boldly unto the throne of grace, that we may obtain mercy, and find grace to help in time of need.

Work Sheet

What is prayer to you? Is it just a religious thing that you do, or are you really expecting God to hear you and answer your prayers?

_____
_____
_____
_____

Do you address God as your Heavenly Father? Have you developed a Father-child mentality with Him? If you are born again, He wants you to call Him 'Father.' Develop this practice!

_____
_____

Do you feel guilty or unworthy to stand before God in prayer? Perhaps you keep looking at your shortcomings or places where you missed the mark in the past. Remember that, in Christ Jesus, you are now right with God through His shed blood. And if you have missed the mark, just confess your sins, believe He has forgiven you, and come before Him without condemnation

Read 2Corinthians 5: 17-21, 1John 1:9 & Isaiah 43:26 and believe!

Specific Kinds Of Prayer

Chapter Two
WHY PRAY

Prayer is the sweetest thing in the world!

Prayer is speaking with the Father and making requests of Him. Prayer is seeking Him earnestly in order that we may be closer to Him and walk more intimately with Him. Prayer is consecrating and dedicating ourselves to His will, plan and purpose for our lives. There is not just one way to pray. There are various ways to commune with Him. But why pray? Particularly, why make requests of the Father? After all, the Lord Jesus already said that He knows what things we have need of. (Read Matthew 6: 7-8) So why pray if He already knows what we are going to ask for? The answer lies in a truth revealed in the Word that is so endearing and wonderful. God literally wants us to invite Him into our affairs.

Free Will

When the Lord created man, He gave man-kind a free will. It is given as a gift, and with that free will comes enormous privilege and tremendous responsibility.

God literally gave to humanity the ability to decide his or her fate and eternal destiny. It is not up to God whether a person embraces His purpose or not. It is up to us. We have to decide and choose God's ways. This powerful thing called 'the will' is the very reason why we must pray if God is going to get intimately involved in our affairs. He gave us that free will and He respects it. If we want Him in our lives, we will have to invite Him in as Lord. If we want Him to be involved in our affairs, we will have to petition Him for Him to get involved. Prayer is how we invite God into our lives and into our affairs.

Prayer is His invitation to intervene on our behalf or on behalf of our loved ones. Prayer releases Him to do in us, for us and through us what we desire to be done – in accordance with His plan and purpose. Prayer is necessary because God will never override our wills. He knows what we have need of. However, He is waiting on us to ask Him so that He can move on our behalf because He has received that invitation from us to do so. Look at the following scripture:

Deuteronomy 30:19
19 I call heaven and earth to record this day against you, that I have set before you life and death, blessing and cursing: therefore choose life, that both thou and thy seed may live:

God gave us the will and ability to choose. It is up to us to allow Him to have His way in our lives. It is up to us to allow Him to get involved in our lives, in our situations and circumstances. He will not force Himself upon us. We must choose to let Him in. We do this through prayer!

Work Sheet

Why do you pray?

_____
_____
_____
_____

Do you understand that you really need God to be your Source in every area of your life?

_____
_____
_____

Do you realize that you have a responsibility to pray, that God is limited as to what He can do in your life unless you give Him access? Explain your answer using the Word of God and the chapter you just read as your reference point

_____
_____
_____
_____

Chapter Three
WHAT TO PRAY FOR

The scriptures give us the right to ask of God, fully expecting Him to respond. God wants to answer your prayers on a consistent basis.

He said that if we ask for anything according to His will, He will hear us and we can be assured that what we ask is granted. Our part is to ask according to His will. **HIS WILL IS REVEALED IN HIS WORD. HIS WORD IS HIS WILL!**

1John 5: 14-15
14 And this is the confidence that we have in him, that, if we ask any thing according to his will, he heareth us: And if we know that he hear us, whatsoever we ask, we know that we have the petitions that we desired of him.

If we want to know what God's will is in any given circumstance or situation, we need to search the scriptures and see what Father has to say. What His

Word says is what Father is saying. His Word is Him speaking to us. He and His Word are One!

What Does The Word Say?

Here are things we can pray about, expecting God to hear us and answer our prayers.

    A. We can ask for help and mercy in our time of testing.

Hebrews 4: 15-16
15 For we have not an high priest which cannot be touched with the feeling of our infirmities; but was in all points tempted like as we are, yet without sin.
16 Let us therefore come boldly unto the throne of grace, that we may obtain mercy, and find grace to help in time of need.

    B. We can ask for God's wisdom when we are facing tests and trials.

James 1: 2-8
2 My brethren, count it all joy when ye fall into divers temptations;
3 Knowing this, that the trying of your faith worketh patience.
4 But let patience have her perfect work, that ye may be perfect and entire, wanting nothing.
5 If any of you lack wisdom, let him ask of God, that giveth to all men liberally, and upbraideth not; and it shall be given him.

6 But let him ask in faith, nothing wavering. For he that wavereth is like a wave of the sea driven with the wind and tossed.
7 For let not that man think that he shall receive any thing of the Lord.
8 A double minded man is unstable in all his ways.

    C. We can ask for forgiveness if we miss the mark and sin.

1John 1:9
9 If we confess our sins, he is faithful and just to forgive us our sins, and to cleanse us from all unrighteousness. (See also 1John 2: 1-2)

    D. We can ask for spiritual wisdom and revelation of God's Word and ways.

Ephesians 1: 15-19
16 Cease not to give thanks for you, making mention of you in my prayers;
17 That the God of our Lord Jesus Christ, the Father of glory, may give unto you the spirit of wisdom and revelation in the knowledge of him:
18 The eyes of your understanding being enlightened; that ye may know what is the hope of his calling, and what the riches of the glory of his inheritance in the saints,
19 And what is the exceeding greatness of his power to us-ward who believe, according to the working of his mighty power,

20 Which he wrought in Christ, when he raised him from the dead, and set him at his own right hand in the heavenly places,
21 Far above all principality, and power, and might, and dominion, and every name that is named, not only in this world, but also in that which is to come:
22 And hath put all things under his feet, and gave him to be the head over all things to the church,
23 Which is his body, the fulness of him that filleth all in all.

> E. We can ask for spiritual strengthening and a deeper walk with God.

Ephesians 3: 14-21
14 For this cause I bow my knees unto the Father of our Lord Jesus Christ,
15 Of whom the whole family in heaven and earth is named,
16 That he would grant you, according to the riches of his glory, to be strengthened with might by his Spirit in the inner man;
17 That Christ may dwell in your hearts by faith; that ye, being rooted and grounded in love,
18 May be able to comprehend with all saints what is the breadth, and length, and depth, and height;
19 And to know the love of Christ, which passeth knowledge, that ye might be filled with all the fulness of God.

20 Now unto him that is able to do exceeding abundantly above all that we ask or think, according to the power that worketh in us,
21 Unto him be glory in the church by Christ Jesus throughout all ages, world without end. Amen.

    F. We can ask for our needs.

Philippians 4:19
19 But my God shall supply all your need according to his riches in glory by Christ Jesus.

    G. We can ask for an out-pouring of God's Spirit.

James 5:7
7 Be patient therefore, brethren, unto the coming of the Lord. Behold, the husbandman waiteth for the precious fruit of the earth, and hath long patience for it, until he receive the early and latter rain. (See also Acts 2: 16-18)

    H. We can ask for our desires.

Mark 11:24
24 Therefore I say unto you, What things soever ye desire, when ye pray, believe that ye receive them, and ye shall have them.

    I. We can ask for direction and Divine guidance.

Specific Kinds Of Prayer

Proverbs 3: 5-6
5 Trust in the LORD with all thine heart; and lean not unto thine own understanding.
6 In all thy ways acknowledge him, and he shall direct thy paths.

> J. We can cast our worries and cares on the Lord.

1Peter 5:7 (AMPC)
7 Casting the whole of your care [all your anxieties, all your worries, all your concerns, once and for all] on Him, for He cares for you affectionately and cares about you watchfully.
(See also Philippians 4: 4-6)

> K. We can pray for the leaders of our country.

1Timothy 2: 1-5
1 I exhort therefore, that, first of all, supplications, prayers, intercessions, and giving of thanks, be made for all men;
2 For kings, and for all that are in authority; that we may lead a quiet and peaceable life in all godliness and honesty.
3 For this is good and acceptable in the sight of God our Saviour;
4 Who will have all men to be saved, and to come unto the knowledge of the truth.
5 For there is one God, and one mediator between God and men, the man Christ Jesus; (See also Romans 13: 1-7)

> L. We can pray for our spiritual leaders.

1 Thessalonians 5:25
25 Brethren, pray for us.

> M. We can pray for the sick. (Read James 5: 13-16)

James 5: 13-16
13 Is any among you afflicted? let him pray. Is any merry? let him sing psalms.
14 Is any sick among you? let him call for the elders of the church; and let them pray over him, anointing him with oil in the name of the Lord:
15 And the prayer of faith shall save the sick, and the Lord shall raise him up; and if he have committed sins, they shall be forgiven him.
16 Confess your faults one to another, and pray one for another, that ye may be healed. The effectual fervent prayer of a righteous man availeth much. (See also Mark 16: 15-20)

> N. We can pray for each other.

Ephesians 6:18
18 Praying always with all prayer and supplication in the Spirit, and watching thereunto with all perseverance and supplication for all saints;

> O. We can pray that we be filled with the knowledge of His will in all wisdom and spiritual understanding.

Colossians 1: 9-12
9 For this cause we also, since the day we heard it, do not cease to pray for you, and to desire that ye might be filled with the knowledge of his will in all wisdom and spiritual understanding;
10 That ye might walk worthy of the Lord unto all pleasing, being fruitful in every good work, and increasing in the knowledge of God;
11 Strengthened with all might, according to his glorious power, unto all patience and longsuffering with joyfulness;
12 Giving thanks unto the Father, which hath made us meet to be partakers of the inheritance of the saints in light:

> P. We can pray that we stand perfect and complete in all the will of God for our lives.

Colossians 4:12
12 Epaphras, who is one of you, a servant of Christ, saluteth you, always labouring fervently for you in prayers, that ye may stand perfect and complete in all the will of God. (See also Hebrews 13: 20-21)

> Q. We can pray that God keep us from falling, to keep us until the day of redemption.

Notice this verse from the Book of Jude.
Jude 24
24 Now unto him that is able to keep you from falling, and to present you faultless before the presence of his glory with exceeding joy,

R. We can worship God, drawing near to Him.

John 4:23-24
23 But the hour cometh, and now is, when the true worshippers shall worship the Father in spirit and in truth: for the Father seeketh such to worship him.
24 God is a Spirit: and they that worship him must worship him in spirit and in truth.

S. We can pray for protection.

Psalm 91: 9-11
9 Because thou hast made the LORD, which is my refuge, even the most High, thy habitation;
10 There shall no evil befall thee, neither shall any plague come nigh thy dwelling.
11 For he shall give his angels charge over thee, to keep thee in all thy ways.

T. We can pray and thank God for sweet sleep and safety as we sleep. (Glory to God)!

Psalm 4:8
8 I will both lay me down in peace, and sleep: for thou, LORD, only makest me dwell in safety.

U. We can pray and commune with God.

2Corinthians 13:13 (AMPC)

14 The grace (favor and spiritual blessing) of the Lord Jesus Christ and the love of God and the presence and fellowship (the communion and sharing together, and participation) in the Holy Spirit be with you all. Amen (so be it).

V. We can pray for peace of mind, regardless of the circumstances.

Philippians 4: 6-7
6 Be careful for nothing; but in every thing by prayer and supplication with thanksgiving let your requests be made known unto God.
7 And the peace of God, which passeth all understanding, shall keep your hearts and minds through Christ Jesus.

W. We can pray for God's desires for us to become our desires so that He can give us the desires of our hearts.

Psalm 37: 4-5 (AMPC)
4 Delight yourself also in the Lord, and He will give you the desires and secret petitions of your heart.
5 Commit your way to the Lord [roll and repose each care of your load on Him]; trust (lean on, rely on, and be confident) also in Him and He will bring it to pass.

X. We can pray for a fresh anointing of God's Holy Spirit.

Psalm 92:10
10 But my horn shalt thou exalt like the horn of an unicorn: I shall be anointed with fresh oil.

Y. We can pray for the infilling of the Spirit.

Luke 11:13
13 If ye then, being evil, know how to give good gifts unto your children: how much more shall your heavenly Father give the Holy Spirit to them that ask him?

Z. We can pray for good things from God.

Matthew 7:11
11 If ye then, being evil, know how to give good gifts unto your children, how much more shall your Father which is in heaven give good things to them that ask him?

While this list may seem long, the truth is that there are many more promises in the Word of God for us to pray and claim because of Jesus. He has provided salvation, healing, deliverance, safety, preservation and soundness for us. Glory to God!

He has given us all things that pertain to life and godliness. However, it is through the knowledge of

God that we learn of the great and precious promises He has provided. Get in the Word daily. Feed upon the Word as your daily bread. Give the Holy Spirit the opportunity to reveal the will and ways of God to your heart. As His will is unveiled, you will have faith to believe God for whatever you may have need of or desire!

2Peter 1: 3-4
3 According as his divine power hath given unto us all things that pertain unto life and godliness, through the knowledge of him that hath called us to glory and virtue:
4 Whereby are given unto us exceeding great and precious promises: that by these ye might be partakers of the divine nature, having escaped the corruption that is in the world through lust.

Work Sheet

Write down John 15:7 and read it over and over. Meditate upon it until it speaks to your heart. Write it here:

_____
_____
_____
_____
_____

Write down a list of five things the Word says you can pray for. Place a scripture verse by each promise.

_____
_____
_____
_____
_____

Will you commit to praying the prayer found in Ephesians 1: 17-19 daily for a Spirit of wisdom and revelation? Will you commit to praying it for yourself and for other believers as well? Write it down here.

_____
_____
_____
_____
_____

Specific Kinds Of Prayer

Chapter Four
HOW TO PRAY SPECIFICALLY

While some may take it for granted that people know or should know how to pray, there are those who desire to be shown how practically. This chapter is written for you if you fit into that category.

Now, how can one know if he or she fits into that category? Are your prayers being answered? Then perhaps you are not formatting your prayers in line with the will of God – the Word of God! Are you having difficulty praying for specific things? Then this chapter is for you. Are you unsure of how to petition God in your natural language or vernacular, so you only pray in tongues? While praying in tongues is extremely valuable and so valuable that we shall give an entire chapter to its study, you should also be praying in your natural language as well, using the Word of God as your guide and the Name of Jesus as your authority. I am not in any way speaking negatively about praying in tongues.

However, I have seen people who prayed that way because they were uncomfortable when it came to praying in English, or their natural language. We should be praying both ways, according to scripture.

1Corinthians 14:15
15 What is it then? I will pray with the spirit, and I will pray with the understanding also: I will sing with the spirit, and I will sing with the understanding also.

In this chapter, I will give examples of how to pray various kinds of prayer based upon some of the ones we spoke of in the previous chapter.

I give these examples not for you to pray them word for word. That would be good and fine if you need or desire to do so. However, these are examples of how to pray in line with God's Word so that you may learn how to approach the Throne of His Grace and receive answers from Heaven. Yes, God still answers prayer. And He desires to answer your prayers.

As we saw previously, if we pray according to His will, we can have the assurance that we have been heard and know that it is done and the answer is on its way to manifestation. I have experienced God answering my prayers requests and humble petitions over and over through the years. Perhaps the examples I give will help and assist you as you seek His Face. While this particular prayer may not have been listed above, it is the most important prayer an individual can ever pray.

How To Pray For Salvation

"Oh God in heaven, I come to you in the name of your Son, the Lord Jesus Christ. Your Word declares that the person who comes to you, you will not cast away (John 6:37). So I know that you receive me now. I believe Jesus died for me and shed His precious and holy blood to wash away my sins. I believe that you raised Him from the dead, and right now, I receive Jesus Christ as my Lord and personal Savior. Jesus is my Lord.

God, you said in your Word that if I do this I would be saved (Romans 10:9-10). So I now confess and boldly declare, according to God's Word, I am saved. I am born again. I am a child of God (John 1:12). Thank you Father for receiving me, saving me, and making me a new creation in Christ Jesus (2 Corinthians 5:17). In Jesus Name I pray, amen."

How To Pray To Be Filled With The Holy Spirit

Heavenly Father, I come to You in the Name of Your Son, the Lord Jesus Christ, my Lord and my Savior. I thank You that I am Your child and that You are my Wonderful Father. I see in Your Word that it is Your will that I be filled with Your Holy Spirit. You said that I am to ask You for the Holy Spirit. I know that He lives in me at salvation. Now I desire to be filled with Him. Your Word says that if I ask You for the Holy Spirit, You will give me the Holy Spirit, and that I can be assured of this. Therefore, I humbly ask You to fill me with Your Holy Spirit in Jesus Name. And because I know that You have said You will fill me, I receive the fullness of Your Holy Spirit now in Jesus Name. Thank You Father for filling me with Your Spirit. Father, I see in Your Word, that when others were initially filled with the Holy Spirit, they spoke with other tongues as the Spirit gave them utterance. The Holy Spirit is the same. When He has done then, He will do now. So, I fully expect to speak with tongues as He gives me the utterance. Thank You Father. Thank You for filling me with the Holy Spirit in Jesus Name. **(Continue to praise the Lord until you sense that utterance coming up from within. As the river of tongues flows up, open your mouth and yield to the Spirit of God. Speak out that supernatural language).**

How To Pray For Your Healing

Heavenly Father, In Jesus Name I approach Your Throne of mercy and grace. I thank You so much that I am Your child, and that You are my very own Wonderful Heavenly Father. I thank You that in your great plan of redemption You have provided healing and Divine health through the sacrifice of Your Son, the Lord Jesus Christ, my Kinsman Redeemer, just like You provided salvation for me. Himself took my infirmities and bore my sicknesses. (Matthew 8:17, Isaiah 53: 1-10 & 1Peter 2:24) I believe that He bore my own so I do not have to bear them. I also believe that His stripes bought and purchased my healing. Father, I chose to believe Your Word. I chose to believe that He was wounded for my transgression, that He was bruised for my iniquities. I believe that the chastisement of my peace was upon Jesus and with His stripes I was healed. If I was healed, I am healed now, according to Your Word. I receive my healing in Jesus Name. And in the authority of His Name, I command all pain, sickness and disease to leave my body, which is His temple, now! I receive my healing now. It's already been purchased. I receive now. And now Father, I lift my hands and praise and worship You that I am healed, I am well and I am whole. I am not moved by what I see or how I feel. I am moved only by what I believe. And I believe God's Word. By His stripes, I was healed. If I was healed, I am healed. Thank You Father in Jesus Name! **(Continue to worship Him believing that it is done).**

How To Pray For Your Desires

Heavenly Father, I come to You in Jesus Name. I thank You so much that You my Wonderful Father and that I am Your child. Father I come to You based upon Your promise in Mark 11:24. Father, Jesus said, "What things soever I desire." Father I desire _____. The Lord Jesus also said, "When I pray." I am praying now. I am asking You for _____. Your word says, "When I pray, believe that I receive them." Therefore, Father, I believe right now that I receive what I have asked for. I believe that I receive _____.

Therefore, I praise You and thank You that what I have asked for now, by faith. I believe that I have it now. I thank You that I believe I have it now. You said that if I believe that I receive, I shall have it. I believe that I have it and I give You thanks for you, in Jesus Name. **(Continue to praise God for what you have prayed for like you already have it. Don't ask for it anymore. Just give thanks like it is already done, according to Mark 11:24. God is faithful)!**

How To Pray For Problems / Cares

*Heavenly Father, I come to You in the Name of Your Holy Son, the Lord Jesus Christ, my Lord and my Savior. I come because my heart is burdened and I need Your help. You are my Rock and I need You. I come on the basis of Your Word. You said that I am not to fret or have any anxiety concerning anything, but that in everything I am to pray and supplicate. I humble myself before You Almighty God, my Father. Your Word says in 1Peter 5:7 that I am to cast all of my worries, all of my anxieties, all of my concerns, once and for all on You, for You care for me affectionately, and care about me watchfully. Your Eyes are on me, My Father. I am the apple of Your Eye. You care for me. You are my Strength and my High Tower. I run into You and I am safe. According to Your Word, I come to You Father. I cast my care on You. I need You to _____.
Intervene in this situation for me, My Father, for You are my Source and in You do I trust. I place this matter in Your Hands, according to Your Word. I cast the care on You now and I leave it with You.*

Thank You Lord for intervening. Thank You for answering. Thank You for taking my cares, my worries and my anxiety. You have them now. Therefore, I refuse to worry or carry care. Instead, I rejoice in You and thank You for what You are doing and what You shall do. Thank You. Thank You. Thank You Father, in Jesus Name, Amen!

How To Pray The Prayer Of Agreement

In my book, *'How To Pray And Get Results,'* I speak of various kinds of prayer that are in the Word of God. One of those kinds of prayer is the Prayer of Agreement. Jesus Himself spoke of the power of this kind of prayer when He said,

Matthew 18: 19-20
19 Again I say unto you, That if two of you shall agree on earth as touching any thing that they shall ask, it shall be done for them of my Father which is in heaven.
20 For where two or three are gathered together in my name, there am I in the midst of them.

What a powerful guarantee from our Lord!

While we have not mentioned this kind of praying in the previous chapter, I would like to show you how this kind of prayer is prayed so that you may also enjoy its tremendous and marvelous benefits. My wife and I prayed this way for our children. We received from the Lord exactly what we agreed in prayer for. This kind of prayer is dynamic in its workings. God answers prayer. In this kind of prayer is also united prayer – a local assembly or a group of believers in prayer and agreement. However, it can be two or three people in agreement just as our Lord said. The key here is to have agreement between you and the person agreeing with you in prayer. In other words, the two, three or more people who you are asking to stand in faith with you concerning a matter needs to know what is being prayed about. That is number one. You do not need anyone agreeing with you who does not agree with you. Second, each of you must know what the Word of God has to say in regard to what is being prayed. You must have the promise of God on the matter. This gives a strong and firm basis for being assured of an answer to prayer. Once you have the Word on the issue, here is how this prayer is prayed:

Dear Heavenly Father, we come to You in the Name of Your Son and our Lord and Savior, the Lord Jesus Christ. We thank You for Your lovingkindness and Your tender mercies which are ours. We thank You our Father for Your promises. We come to You concerning _____. Father, Your Word says, _____. Therefore, we come in agreement, asking You to _____. Now Father, You said that if two or more of us agree on earth concerning anything that we shall ask, it shall be done. Father we are on earth and we are in agreement concerning what we are asking. You said, "It shall be done." Thank You Father. We believe

You. Therefore, we believe it is done and we count in done. And we give You the glory for it, in Jesus Name, Amen!

Continual Prayers

There are prayers that can and should be prayed continually! We shall list a few of them here.

These kinds of prayer are necessary, for some of them are a part of a process. For instance, some of them are concerning spiritual growth, which is a process. Here is one of those types of prayer.

How To Pray For Wisdom & Revelation From God's Word

I heard a man of God who has gone to be with Jesus speak of praying this particular prayer that is written in the scriptures.

He said that he prayed it constantly, sometimes twice a day. And one day, revelation knowledge of God's Word became alive within him. So much so that he asked his wife, "What in the world have I been preaching?" The Word of God was unveiled to him in tremendous and life-transforming fashion. I heard him speak of this over thirty years ago. And for that length of time, I have also been praying the following prayer. It has resulted in the Word of God being revealed within me and to me on a consistent basis. This will work for any sincere believer who is earnest and diligent to pray it constantly. I advise that you pray it daily. Before I show you how I learned to pray it, let's look at again at a prayer the Apostle Paul prayed for the saints at Ephesus.

Ephesians 1: 15-21
15 Wherefore I also, after I heard of your faith in the Lord Jesus, and love unto all the saints,
16 Cease not to give thanks for you, making mention of you in my prayers;
17 That the God of our Lord Jesus Christ, the Father of glory, may give unto you the spirit of wisdom and revelation in the knowledge of him:
18 The eyes of your understanding being enlightened; that ye may know what is the hope of his calling, and what the riches of the glory of his inheritance in the saints,
19 And what is the exceeding greatness of his power to us-ward who believe, according to the working of his mighty power,
20 Which he wrought in Christ, when he raised him from the dead, and set him at his own right hand in the heavenly places,
21 Far above all principality, and power, and might, and dominion, and every name that is named, not only in this world, but also in that which is to come:
22 And hath put all things under his feet, and gave him to be the head over all things to the church,
23 Which is his body, the fulness of him that filleth all in all.

The Apostle Paul said that he prayed this way for these saints! It is an anointed prayer and one that we should pray often for ourselves and even for fellow believers in Christ Jesus. Here is how I pray it for myself and how I pray it for God's people.

"God of my Lord Jesus Christ, Father of glory, give to me the Spirit of wisdom and revelation in the knowledge of You. Let the eyes of my understanding be enlightened that I may know what is the hope of Your calling, and what is the riches of the glory of Your inheritance in the saints, and what is the exceeding greatness of Your power towards us who believe, according to the working of Your mighty power which You wrought in Christ Jesus when you raised Him from the dead, and set Him at Your own right hand in the heavenly places, far above all principality, and power and might and dominion, and every name that is named, not only in this world, but also in that which is to come: And has put all things under His feet, and gave Him to be the head over all things to the church, which is His body, the fullness of Him that fills all in all. I ask for this, and thank You for it Father. I believe I receive in Jesus Name, amen."

Now this prayer is for spiritual growth! I pray this particular prayer to receive wisdom, insight and understanding of God's Word.

The knowledge of His Word is progressive. So this prayer can (and should) be prayed daily so that one can receive more and more light and revelation. Our growth in the Lord is a process. Therefore, this prayer can be prayed at greater and greater levels, resulting in greater and deeper insights and revelations of God's precious Word – bringing us into more and more profound levels of freedom in Christ, higher comprehensions of spiritual authority in prayer and practice, and more and more intimacy with the Father God!

Here is another one we can continually pray:

How To Pray For A Deeper Walk With The Lord

I have been praying this prayer constantly for over thirty years. And I am constantly receiving revelation and insight into God's Word. His Word is alive within me and literally explodes within my being on an on-going basis. Praying this way will greatly benefit your walk with God as well.

Again, it is written in the writings of the Apostle Paul. He got on his knees and prayed it for the saints at Ephesus. By the way, while we can pray it without kneeling, it is good and acceptable for us to follow his example and pray it sometimes upon our knees as well. Kneeling before the Lord shows that we reverence Him and respect Him as God – the Creator of the universe, and our Sovereign Lord and Source. Kneeling before Him in humility, with the awareness that we need Him, shows that we honor God! Therefore, sometimes it is good to kneel for we are in the Presence of the Most High God! This prayer is found in Ephesians chapter three, verse fourteen to twenty-one. Please read it again. But here is how I personalize and pray it for myself.

For this cause, I bow my knees unto the Father of my Lord Jesus Christ, of Whom the whole family in heaven and earth is named. Father, grant unto me, according to the riches of Your glory, that I may be strengthened with might by Your Holy Spirit in my inner man. May Christ reign in my heart by faith, that I being rooted and grounded in love, may be able to comprehend with all saints what is the breadth and length and depth and height (of your love). And that I may experience for myself the love of Christ, which passes mere knowledge without experience, that I may become a body wholly filled and flooded with all the fullness of God, and may have the richest measure of the Divine Presence. Now unto the Father Who is able to do exceeding abundantly above all that I ask or think, according to the power which works in me, Unto the Father be glory in the church and in my life, by Christ Jesus, throughout all ages, world without end, in Jesus Name I humbly pray, and I thank You Father in His Name, Amen!

I usually pray verse nineteen of this chapter using the words from the *Amplified Bible Classic Edition*. I just love how it sounds. It grips my spirit).

How To Pray For Your Leaders Of Your Nation

As we have seen in the previous chapter, we have a God-given responsibility to pray for the leaders of our nation. Whether we like them or not, whether we approve of them or not; whether they are saved or not, we have been authorized by Almighty God to pray for them. This kind of praying is also to be done continually. Here is one we can pray for our Nation's leaders. The main way to pray for them is to be led by the Spirit of God. But this is a good starting point and a way that we can pray on a consistent basis.

Father of our Lord Jesus Christ, we thank You for the leader of our Nation. We thank You for the Prime Minister. (Or whatever you may call the leader of your Nation). We thank You for the deputy Prime Minister. We thank You for the Cabinet and for all those in authority in this land. We pray for them. We pray for the Commissioner of the Police Force and the Commodore of the Defense Force (you may say for your Armed Forces, etc). We ask You to bless them. Grant them wisdom and insight so that they would lead the country in and walk in accordance with Your will for this country. Bless them with protection and with Your anointing as they carry out their duties and responsibilities. Thank You Father for this, In Jesus Mighty Name. Amen!

How To Pray For An Out-pouring Of God's Spirit

Father God, I thank You for Your loving-kindness and Your tender mercies. I thank You for Your Word. Father, many people need Your Son. They need the Lord Jesus Christ in their lives. They are being destroyed by the enemy. They are being deceived and misled by various kinds of lusts and evil. We cannot reach them apart from Your Holy Spirit. You said in Your Word that no one can come to Jesus except You draw them. (See John 6:37) Father, just our preaching or teaching alone will not do. Without the power of Your Spirit upon what we preach or teach, it has no life, no substance. We need Your Holy Spirit moving in our lives. We need Your Holy Spirit moving in our ministries. We need Your anointing. We need His power flowing as mighty rivers of living water in order to reach more and more people with the saving, healing delivering power of the Lord Jesus Christ. God, we see in Your Word that You have promised to pour out of Your Spirit in the last days. Father, You did not say, "Last day," as only on the Day of Pentecost, but, "Last Days," showing that You still desire to pour out of Your Holy Spirit today. Father, You said to ask You for rain in the time of the latter rain. You said that You are waiting for the precious fruit of the earth. You are waiting on a harvest. Father, the rain of Your Spirit is necessary in order to bring in that harvest. In Jesus Name, in the Name of Your Son, I am asking You for the rain of Your Spirit. I am asking You to pour out of Your Spirit upon Your sons and daughters, and upon Your servants and hand-maidens. May Your Spirit manifest Himself in our midst. May He manifest His gifts, administrations and operations in Jesus Name! Let there be marvels and miracles, signs and wonders. Stretch forth Your Hands to heal in Jesus Name. Manifest Your glory, God. Let Your Presence and Your power be known in the earth, even in our day, even in this time. Father, we ask for these things, in the Name of Jesus Christ, Your Son, for His honor and for His glory. And for these things we give You thanks and praise, in Jesus Wonderful, Worthy and Majestic Name, Amen!

There is more to pray in this manner. Repentance is necessary as well. Humbling ourselves before the Lord is also necessary. The prayer above is just to serve as a starting point and example. In all, one must be led by the Spirit in the prayer life. So look to Him for guidance so that you can pray what needs to be prayed so that Heaven can invade earth in mighty power, to the glory of King Jesus Christ!

Work Sheet

What did the Lord Jesus say regarding praying in faith? Write it out here.

_____
_____
_____
_____

When are you to believe you receive, according to Jesus?

_____
_____

What is the proper response if you believe you receive?

_____

Write down a desire of your heart. Then pray as directed in the chapter. Believe you receive and give thanks continually as if your request was granted when you prayed. Do so until the prayer manifest. Then come back to what you wrote down and write the words 'DONE' next to it.

_____
_____

Specific Kinds Of Prayer

Chapter Five
ASSURED OF AN ANSWER

John 15:7
7 If ye abide in me, and my words abide in you, ye shall ask what ye will, and it shall be done unto you.

What is real prayer? It is taking Father's Word back to Him, reminding Him of His promises, fully expecting Him to keep His Word and do as He said He will do. This is what He desires from each of His children. He wants us to believe Him!

Jesus our Lord gave us the Word as the basis for answered prayer. This takes the mystery away. There are those who believe that God just answers the prayers that He chooses to answer. They pray with no faith, no belief that He will respond to their requests. They just do so because they were traditionally taught to pray and *see* if God answers. He may, or in most cases, He may not. Then there may be others who believe that God always answers prayer, however, we should never expect Him to always do too much, for sometimes He says, *"Yes,"* sometimes He says, *"No,"* and at other times He says, *"Wait."* Have you ever heard that? This kind of thinking says, *"Don't expect too much when you pray, because you never know what God will do."* While it is true that we may never comprehend exactly how God will do what He has promised to do for those who choose to believe Him and trust Him; and while it is true that patience is a part of the process in regard to answered prayer, please understand that we can know with assurance that God will keep His Word to us. Prayer is not based upon a wish. According to the words of our Lord Jesus Christ, it is based upon a guarantee!

Jesus gave us the secret to having our prayers answered. He said that we must abide in Him and His Word must abide within us. He guaranteed that if we do, when we pray, Heaven will respond and in our favor. The question is never, *"Does God answer prayer?"* The question is never, *"Does God answer all prayer?"* The real question is, **"Are we abiding in Jesus, and is His Word (the promises of God) abiding in us?"** God answers our prayers when the conditions are met!

Living The Abiding Life

Seeing that this is so – and it is so, for Jesus Himself said so – let us consider the keys to having our prayers continually answered more efficiently, so that we can experience the fulfillment of His promises in our lives more effectively. First, let us consider the two principles, (keys or qualifications), for answered prayer. Here they are:

1. **Jesus said we must abide in Him.**

2. **Jesus said His Words must abide in us.**

What does it mean to abide? According to the **James Strong's Exhaustive Concordance,** the word abide here in John chapter fifteen, verse seven comes from the **Greek** word *Meno*. This word means the following;

- **to stay (in a given place, state, relation or expectancy)**
- **continue**
- **dwell**
- **endure**
- **be present**
- **remain**
- **stand**
- **tarry (for).**

Consider these definitions well!

Our Lord says that if we truly desire to see and be assured of answers to our prayers we must *stay, continue, dwell, endure, be present, remain, stand and tarry for and in Him.* Interestingly, the same Greek word, **Meno,** is used when the Master speaks of His Words (plural) abiding in us. So, just as we are to *stay, continue, dwell, endure, be present,* *remain, stand, and tarry in and for* Jesus, we must also, *stay, continue, dwell, endure, be present, remain, stand and tarry in His Words.* Wow! Ponder these things carefully remembering that this is what guarantees us answers to our prayers. I believe therefore, that it essential that we consider these two qualifications for answered prayer separately. Let us mediate upon the first one together.

Abiding In Jesus

Jesus said, **"If you abide in Me,"**

Are we *"in Him?"* As born again believers, **"YES, WE ARE IN CHRIST JESUS!"** We are in Him because of the work of the Holy Spirit. When we gave our lives to Him, the Blessed Spirit of God washed us from our sins in His precious blood, imparting the very life of God to us, making us new creations in Him. What kind of creations? Righteous creations. He gave us right-standing with the Father, a standing that is indeed powerful and marvelous. We have the standing of sons of God. We are His children, born of Him. (Please read, Romans 5:1-9, 2Corinthians 5:17-21, John 1:12-13, 1Peter 1:23, James 1:18, 1John 5:12-13 and Romans 8:16-17)

Then the Holy Spirit did something else which give us our standing in Him. He miraculously baptized, (or placed us), into that spiritual, supernatural body called the body of Christ.

1Corinthians 12:13
13 For by one Spirit are we all baptized into one body, whether we be Jews or Gentiles, whether we be bond or free; and have been all made to drink into one Spirit.

God saved us, yes! And then He raised us up and made us to sit together in heavenly places in Christ Jesus. We are in Him. The Holy Spirit placed us in Him. He's not going to do this. He already has if you have been born again.

Ephesians 2: 4-6
4 But God, who is rich in mercy, for his great love wherewith he loved us,
5 Even when we were dead in sins, hath quickened us together with Christ, (by grace ye are saved;)
6 And hath raised us up together, and made us sit together in heavenly places in Christ Jesus:

We are literally in Him now!

We are literally in heavenly places in Him now, while we are still on earth. This is the most powerful place to be – in Christ Jesus. We must learn to pray from this place of son-ship and authority. We will get to that in a moment.

We are right now in two places at the same time. *"How can this be?"* one may ask. The answer lies in comprehending that Christ Jesus, after His resurrection from the dead, became the **HEAD** – and – by His Holy Spirit – makes us a part of His body.

Well, wherever the head is, the body is and wherever the body is, the head is. And just as this is so in the natural, it is equally as true in the spirit realm. Our **HEAD**, the Lord Jesus Christ, is in Heaven at the right hand of God the Father. Because we are a part of His body, where He is, we are too. We are in the earth, representing His Kingdom. Therefore, He is where we are for the Head is where the body is. So the Risen Lord fills heaven and earth, for we are one with Him as parts of His body – the true church made up of all who live under His Lordship. Glory to God! The Spirit of God through the Apostle Paul says these words:

Ephesians 1: 19-23
19 And what is the exceeding greatness of his power to us-ward who believe, according to the working of his mighty power,
20 Which he wrought in Christ, when he raised him from the dead, and set him at his own right hand in the heavenly places,
21 Far above all principality, and power, and might, and dominion, and every name that is named, not only in this world, but also in that which is to come:
22 And hath put all things under his feet, and gave him to be the head over all things to the church,
23 Which is his body, the fulness of him that filleth all in all.

How does He fill all in all? He does this through His body. We are the fullness of Jesus. What does that mean? We are a part of Him, a part of His body.

He has chosen to be one with us. We are one spirit with the Lord.

1Corinthians 6:17
17 But he that is joined unto the Lord is one spirit.

The Holy Spirit has done all the hard work for us. He has made us new creations and placed us in Christ Jesus. This is done. Now, beloved, it is up to each of us to consciously make the everyday decision to abide in Him. How does one do that? First, we abide in Him by realizing our utter dependence upon Him. He is the very Source of our lives. This is why He used the analogy of the true Vine and the branches right before He spoke of prayer in verse seven of John chapter fifteen. He has not changed subjects, This is all one context. He is the true Vine, and we are the branches, just as He is the Head and we are the body. The branches cannot live apart from the vine. Their very sustenance comes from the life in the vine. Apart from the vine they cannot survive, they cannot live. Apart from the vine they cannot be all they were created to be, do all they were made to do. They cannot bear fruit for their very sustenance come from the vine.

Likewise, it is vital for us to understand that we cannot be all we are supposed to be and do all we are supposed to do, nor can we bear fruit that pleases God unless we stay united to the Vine, the Lord Jesus Christ. We must remain in union and communion with Him. We must have our dependency upon Him. We need Him. Second, we abide in Him by walking in obedience to Him. Abiding in Him is living under His Lordship, choosing to follow Him in lovingly, worshipful, reverent and humble obedience to His ways.

We are in Him. Now we must stay, continue, dwell, endure, remain and be present in Him by doing as He instructs us to do. After all, He is the Head and we are the body. We should be following His lead. It may help us greatly if we understand that the main message and command of the Master when He was speaking had to do with walking in the New Commandment that He gave to us – the command to love each other as He loved us. This in itself reveals why many prayers do not get answered. People are not walking in obedience to the Head of the body and walking in His love towards fellow-believers. Read from John chapters thirteen through seventeen for yourself and you will see that this is so.

We cannot be confident that our prayers are going to be answered by walking rebelliously, being disobedient to the Head of the church. The enemy will not be able to block the effects of our prayer life if we are walking in His ways. May we all consider this well! Obedience is the key to the blessings of God.

It would help us greatly to read through and meditate in that great chapter on faith in Hebrews eleven again and see the role that obedience played in the lives of the faithful. Beloved, obedience is the highest expression of true faith! If we really believe

God, we will do as He says. There is no faith without obedience!

His Word Abiding In Us

Jesus said, **"And my words abide in you."**

This is the second of the qualifications for answered prayer that our Lord gave. His words must abide in us. This disqualifies some from being assured of answers to their prayers. Many believers do not take time daily to feed upon God's Word. They have yet to learn the importance of the scriptures and its relevance to our lives as Kingdom citizens. We are *'Kingdom Ambassadors.'* We therefore have the responsibility to approach the Throne of Grace with the very language of the King of the Kingdom.

The Master said that if we want our prayers answered, we will have to have His Words abiding within us. Why is this so? Consider this truth as we look once again at something the Spirit of God said through the Apostle John in First John. In the light of what we are studying, this passage will come alive within us as we muse and meditate upon it.

1John 5: 14-15
14 And this is the confidence that we have in him, that, if we ask any thing according to his will, he heareth us:

15 And if we know that he hear us, whatsoever we ask, we know that we have the petitions that we desired of him.

According to this passage, we are told that if we ask anything according to His will, He hears us, and therefore, we can be sure of an answer to our requests – if we pray according to His will. How will we know that we are praying according to His will? Jesus said His words have to abide in us. His Word is His will. His Word reveals His will.

How does one know the will of God in any given matter? Do we look to our emotions? Do we look to our feelings? Do we look to the circumstances or the situations? Do we look to the opinions of others – friends, family, or the experts? No, we look to the Word. We look and see what God has to say in the scriptures. His Word is His will. May God open our eyes to see this glorious truth! When we pray based upon what the Word has to say regarding the situation or circumstance, we can be assured of an answer. **Prayer is taking Father's Word back to Him.** Before we pray, we should take time to search the Word regarding whatever we are dealing with and take two or three days (if possible) to meditate in the Word until the Word speaks to us. I heard a man of God say that he always got answers to his prayers because he always prayed in line with the Word. He said sometimes he would not even pray about the matter right away. He would take a few days and meditate in the Word regarding it. This builds faith, beloved. When we feed continually upon what Father has to say, our confidence in Him soars. The more we do this, the more we are fortified from within regarding God's will concerning the matter. The Word is our connection to the Father. We pray based upon the Word, and whatsoever we ask, we know (even before we see or feel it) that it is done. So, we give God praise, thanksgiving and glory because we know that we know that we know it is a done deal.

Jesus said that His Words have to be abiding in us if we want our prayers to be answered. How can we know if the Word is abiding in us? Here is a truth to consider. When a challenge presents itself, does your heart and mind immediately go to, *"What does God's Word have to say about this?"* If a sickness attempts to latch itself to your body, does your mind and heart say, *"What does God's Word say regarding this?"* If a financial need comes up, does your heart and mind say, *"What does God's Word have to say about this?"* What comes up within you when the pressure is on? That will tell you what is abiding in you in abundance.

Jesus said that it is out of the mouth that a person speaks. When you are under pressure, what is in you is what is going to come to the surface and come out of you. If you face a circumstance and the first thing you do is curse or uses foul language that is what is in you. Now the question becomes, *"How did that get in you?"* Perhaps you were constantly feeding upon it, letting it in. Maybe the movies you watched or the music you listened to, or the company you keep continually use foul language. It got in you from somewhere. You fed on it. It got in. Now how does one get God's Word deeply on the inside so that he or she can be assured of an answer to prayer? The same way! **You must feed on the Word, dig into the Word and meditate in the Word until the Word gets in you in abundance.** You must learn how to listen to and feed on good teachings and ministry of God's Word until the Word gets in you. You must make up your mind that God's Word is important to you and give yourself to the Word. Look at this passage from the Book of Proverbs.

Proverbs 4: 20-22
20 My son, attend to my words; incline thine ear unto my sayings.
21 Let them not depart from thine eyes; keep them in the midst of thine heart.
22 For they are life unto those that find them, and health to all their flesh.

What powerful and life-transforming words!

This literally gives us the keys or principles to ensuring God's Word dwells within us, so that when we pray, we can be assured of answers to our petitions. This is available for each of us. All we have to do is practice daily what God says here.

Since having His Word abiding in us is essential to receiving from the Lord, let us look for a few moments at what this passage is saying. First we are told to *attend to God's Word!* This simply means give attention to what Father has to say. Put God's

Word first in every situation and in every circumstance. We are to put His Word first. We are to look to the Word and make it our number one priority. This does speak of daily diligence! We should be feeding on the Word as our spiritual food, our necessary food. Hear these words from the Prophet Jeremiah and meditate upon them for a moment. They are truly powerful as they show the priority the prophet of God gave to the Word of God.

Jeremiah 15:16
16 Thy words were found, and I did eat them; and thy word was unto me the joy and rejoicing of mine heart: for I am called by thy name, O LORD God of hosts.

Job spoke of esteeming God's Word more than his necessary food.

Job 23:12
12 Neither have I gone back from the commandment of his lips; I have esteemed the words of his mouth more than my necessary food.

The **Hebrew** word for **esteemed** here is the word *tsâphan.* It means to *hide* or to *lay up.* It is the same word that the Psalmist David used when he spoke of hiding God's Word in his heart, so that he might not sin against Him. (See Psalm 119: 9-11)

In essence, it is speaking of God's Word abiding deeply within the inner man. Job held God's Word near and dear to his heart. He deemed it more necessary than his physical food. Has the Word gained that place in imminence and honor in our lives? Only we, as individual believers, can answer that.

Jesus said that we cannot live by bread alone, but by every word that proceeds from the mouth of God. (Matthew 4:4) We simply must put God's Word first in our lives if we desire to see answers to our prayers. Make time each day to feed on His Word and hear what Father has to say. Stop making excuses. Read God's Word daily!

***Next, we are told to* incline our ears to His sayings!**

It seems like most people incline their ears to what everyone else is saying, rather than what God is saying.

To incline our ears means to listen to the Word of God. This is a secret to His Word abiding within us. We are greatly influenced to believe based upon what we pay attention and listen to. Hearing is vitally important, for what we listen to constantly gets down into the core of our being, and greatly affects what we think, believe, say and practice. We live our lives and operate them based upon whatever we allow to dwell in us in great measure. This is why the Bible says, **"Keep thy heart with all diligence; for out of it are the issues of life."** (Proverbs 4:23) In other words, we believe and live our lives based upon what is in our hearts. The word **"*keep*"** here is very interesting in the **Hebrew**. It comes from the word *Natsar*. It actually means *to guard or to protect.* Why would we need to guard or protect our hearts – our spirits and souls? Because whatever we permit to get in there in abundance will control our thinking, believing, and therefore, our very lives.

If we are going to have faith or believe when we pray, (which is essential to receiving from the Lord), we will have to ensure that God's Word – which is the food of faith – dwells deeply within. Jesus said God's Word has to be abiding in us if we are to receive answers from God when we pray. We need to listen to His Word!

This generation is perhaps more blessed than any before it. We literally have no excuses whatsoever for not abiding in God's Word. We can read the Word. We can listen to the Word in audio format – and even listen as our phones read the scriptures to us. We can listen to the Word computers or tablets. We can even watch and behold beautiful scenes and pictures as we listen to the Word. We have no excuse.

Then, we can listen as anointed men and women of God expound the Word to us, whether we are in church, in a meeting, a home-group Bible Study. We can listen to them in audio formats as they teach and preach God's truths. We can feed on God's Word, which builds us up in faith, so that when we pray we pray in faith. Faith pleases God! He can do marvels. He is simply waiting on somebody to believe His Word – to believe His promises. Listening to the

Word continually builds trust and confidence in God, increasing us in understanding and wisdom.

God's Word is no ordinary book. God's Word is the living Word of the Creator, the Almighty God. Our Father's Presence and power are in His Word. And when His Word is fed upon constantly and the Holy Spirit makes His Word alive within us – exploding revelation and spiritual comprehension within our spirits – truth makes us free. Truth elevates our thinking. Truth lifts us up to God's realm, the realm of faith, where all things are truly possible. Here is how the Lord Jesus describes it:

Mark 4:24
24 And he said unto them, Take heed what ye hear: with what measure ye mete, it shall be measured to you: and unto you that hear shall more be given.

I love the Amplified Bible Classic Edition of this particular verse.

Mark 4:24 (AMPC)
24 And He said to them, Be careful what you are hearing. The measure [of thought and study] you give [to the truth you hear] will be the measure [of virtue and knowledge] that comes back to you— and more [besides] will be given to you who hear.

Can your heart take it in?

Do you really want your prayers answered? Jesus said that God's Word has to dwell in you for you to be guaranteed that your petitions will be granted. How can we get the Word to dwell in us continually? By hearing the Word constantly. Jesus said we are to be careful what we are hearing. That sounds like the warning that we read in Proverbs, *to guard our hearts with all diligence* – **with all diligence!** What a powerful statement. **Another translation says, "above all that you guard." (See Proverbs 4:23, AMPC)**

Listen to God's Word. Make time for His Word. You will come to know God through His Word. Your faith will build and grow through His Word. You will pray in line with His will through His Word. And when you pray, God will move on your behalf because His Word is abiding continually in you!

The third step given to us concerning having the Word of God dwelling deeply in our hearts is that we are to **"not let the Word depart from our eyes."** This speaks of reading and studying the Word continually. We are to give ourselves to the Word. There is no substitute for God's Word. Each believer should make time daily to read the scriptures. We should dig into His Word and hear God in His Word. Yes, listening is important; but so is reading and studying the Word for ourselves. We need to be as the saints at Berea who – after listening to the Apostle Paul preach – went and searched the scriptures to make sure that what he was saying was so. (Acts 17:11) We need to know what Father says in the Word so that we can take His Word back to Him in prayer. We are instructed to remind Him. Remind Him of what? Remind Him of what He said. (See Isaiah 43:26)

How can we remind Him if we are not in continual remembrance of what He has promised? Let us therefore make our time in His Word our priority. The Master said that if we want to be assured of an answer to prayer, His Words must abide in us!

Then we are told to keep God's Word in the midst of our hearts. That sounds just like what Jesus said. We are to have God's Word abiding in us. How are we to keep His Word in the midst of our hearts? We do this by attending to the Word; by inclining our ear to His says; and by not letting His Word depart from our eyes. If we practice these three things continually, we will have His Word dwelling richly and deeply within us and can be assured of answers to our prayers. We will pray in line with the Word. This is His will. Therefore, we can be confident that when we practice the principles the Master gave, we shall experience the results He has promised.

John 15:7 (AMPC)
7 If you live in Me [abide vitally united to Me] and My words remain in you and continue to live in your hearts, ask whatever you will, and it shall be done for you.

Specific Kinds Of Prayer

Work Sheet

What two principles did the Lord Jesus Christ give which guarantee answers to prayer?

_____

_____

What does it mean to abide in Jesus?

_____

_____

How can we ensure that God's Word abide in us? What are the principles?

_____

_____

_____

Will you commit to finding out what God's Word has to say in regard to what you desire to pray about so that you can practice praying according to the promises of God from now on, instead of your emotions which lack stability?

_____

_____

_____

Specific Kinds Of Prayer

Chapter Six
HAVE FAITH IN GOD

Faith!

This is what pleases the Lord and what causes Him to move on our behalf. There is no telling what all God will do for those who truly believe Him and act upon His Word. God takes pleasure and great delight in those who choose to believe Him, regardless of what they may presently see or presently feel. Faith pleases Him!

Hebrews 11:6
6 But without faith it is impossible to please him: for he that cometh to God must believe that he is, and that he is a rewarder of them that diligently seek him.

The faith principle is essential to having our prayers answered. To see results, we will have to believe God. Believe Him based upon what? Believe Him based upon His Word – His promises, – what He has said. We will have to look into the Word of

God and pray according to what is written, fully expecting Him to do exactly what He has said that He will do. Faith is taking God at His Word.

In regards to answered prayer, the Lord Jesus Christ Himself said the following words;

Mark 11: 22-26
22 And Jesus answering saith unto them, Have faith in God.
23 For verily I say unto you, That whosoever shall say unto this mountain, Be thou removed, and be thou cast into the sea; and shall not doubt in his heart, but shall believe that those things which he saith shall come to pass; he shall have whatsoever he saith.
24 Therefore I say unto you, What things soever ye desire, when ye pray, believe that ye receive them, and ye shall have them.
25 And when ye stand praying, forgive, if ye have ought against any: that your Father also which is in heaven may forgive you your trespasses.
26 But if ye do not forgive, neither will your Father which is in heaven forgive your trespasses.

Faith Principles

Once again, it is vital to emphasize this point: **Faith pleases God.** We cannot please Him without it. Therefore, if we truly desire to please Him, we shall have to learn how to live by faith, walk by faith and pray in faith!

Specific Kinds Of Prayer

In the passage above, our Lord gives us the principles of faith. He shows us how faith operates, how to operate in faith in prayer, and the greatest hindrance to faith. It had been an interesting few days. The Lord was with His disciples and he was on His way to the temple. He was hungry and seeing a fig tree afar off, He went to get some figs. However, the tree only had leaves. It had no figs. What did Jesus do? He decided to use this as a teachable moment for His disciples, and by extension for us as well. He cursed the fig tree. No, He did not use profanity. He told the tree to die. The Bible says, ***"He said unto it."*** This means that He spoke directly to that tree. What did He say? He said, ***"No man eat fruit of thee, henceforth forever."*** Then He walked away. Wow! Please also notice that He did not speak under His breath either. He spoke aloud, loud enough for all of His disciples to hear Him. Did they see any difference in that tree when the Master spoke those words? Not right away. They did not see any change. As a matter of fact, they went to the temple and then returned where they were staying and they still did not see any change. The Master did not even look to see if that tree was still standing. He did not go and examine it. He did not even speak to it again. As far as He was concerned, it was done. It was finished. That tree had no choice. And the next morning as they headed back to the temple they saw that tree dried up from the root. It was dead! (Read Mark 11: 12-21)

Peter said, ***"Master, behold, the fig tree which thou cursedst is withered away."*** He was astonished and so were the other disciples. This is when Jesus gave them the principles of faith. He spoke of how the principles worked in regard to their words and He spoke of how the principles work in regard to *'petition'* prayers. This is speaking of when we pray for ourselves, for our desires or wants. Praying for others goes by a different set of rules than this particular prayer, for others have their own will. God will not force our will upon the will of others. He gave them the will and He respects their decisions. You should not doubt this for it is easy to prove. It is His will that none perish, but that all come to repentance. (See 2Peter 3:9). Still, many are perishing. Why? They perish because they choose to. They have a will and if a person is to follow Jesus and walk in His ways he or she will have to 'will to.' They will have to decide to!

Likewise, we cannot force our desires upon others in prayer. We can pray that God works within them to bring their desires in line with His will and desires for them. This is a part of intercessory prayer. As it pertains to the principles of faith our Lord taught here, and specifically in regard to answered prayer, Jesus says exactly what we can pray and believe God for.

When Peter said in shock, **"Master, behold the fig tree which You cursed is withered away,"** Jesus did not seem the least bit concerned. He had fully expected it to. He had spoken the command of faith and as far as He was concerned, it had to come to pass. How did Jesus respond? He literally told His

Specific Kinds Of Prayer

disciples that all of mankind has that ability if they will **"have faith in God."** In other words, if we will understand the principles of faith and practice them continually, the Spirit of God will work on our behalf in marvelous and even astounding ways just as He did when our Lord cursed that fig tree. What are these principles of faith the Master taught? While we will only be examining in detail faith as related to prayer, we will mention some of the other aspects of the faith life as well. Remember, faith pleases God and it is impossible to please Him without it.

First, Jesus said that we are to ***"have faith in God."*** While it is true that another way this can be translated is, ***"Have the faith of God,"*** I believe that it is essential that we consider the power in those words as translated in the King James Version of the Scriptures. We are to have faith in God, not in ourselves. We are to trust in the Lord, not in our own selves. In others words, we are to depend upon God as our Source of wisdom, power and strength. We are to lean on and rely upon Him. We are to look to Him to help us, provide for us and to keep us. We are to depend upon Him to answer our prayers and to do the things He has promised to do. And we are also to depend upon Him to move our mountains – those undesirable things that are attempting to bring destruction or harm in our lives. This brings us to the second principle of faith as taught by the Master. Jesus said that if we speak to that mountain standing in our way, (whatever it may be, whether sickness, disease, fear, lack, or even a storm), commanding it to be removed – believing that what we say shall come to pass – it shall be done for us, just as He spoke to that fig tree, commanding it to die and it did. Jesus said that! Jesus said that! He said that the faith principle of speaking to whatever may be hindering you or aiming to cause you harm, commanding things to change, you shall have what you say.

Now, who is going to ensure that your words come to pass? Go back to verse twenty-two – **"have faith in God!"** The Spirit of God will bring your words to pass just as He brought the words of the Master to pass. He made that tree dry up from the roots in response to the command of Jesus. And if we will believe and speak words in line with God's Word against anything the enemy tries against us, with our faith in God's power – not our power – the Spirit of God will bring our words to pass as well. These truths are pointed out in verses twenty-two and twenty-three of Mark chapter eleven.

There is much that can be said along these lines. However, let us consider the next principle of faith Jesus gave us in relation to prayer. He tells us how to get them answered. Ponder this carefully. Jesus said, **"Therefore I say unto you, What things soever ye desire, when ye pray, believe that ye receive them, and ye shall have them."** (See Mark 11:24) What is that therefore there for? It is there because the key to both verse twenty-three and twenty-four of Mark chapter eleven is rooted in what Jesus said in verse twenty-two when He said, **"Have faith in God."** We must have faith in God when we speak to those mountains in our way, believing and expecting Him to move them or ensure that they move on our behalf, and we must have faith in God that when we pray, He will respond. It's a matter of faith!

How is faith shown in relation to prayer? Jesus said, when we pray for whatever we desire, we are to believe that we receive. Now this explains why many have not received answers to their prayers. They did not believe they received when they prayed. They were waiting to receive before they believe. But where is the faith in that? We do not need to believe we receive after we receive for we already have the manifestation of what we were praying for. We need to believe we receive **_when_** we pray!

Faith in prayer is actually believing that God heard us, believing that He has answered, and believing that what we have requested (our desire) is granted, before we may even see, feel or experience it. Faith is believing!

Now someone may say, *"I can't believe I receive something and that I have it, when I have not seen it, or felt it. How can I believe I receive healing when I still feel sick? How can I believe I receive the money I asked for when the bill has not been paid yet? How can I believe I receive what I have asked for before I see it?"* That is how faith works. Faith trusts God and trusts Him so much that the person of faith chooses to believe that their petition or request is granted, and gives God thanks and glory as if they already have – in experience – what they are standing in faith for. They believe that the moment they asked God for whatever they desire, it is done. They believe God heard, therefore, it is a done deal.

I have seen God answer my prayers as I stood on this wonderful promise from Jesus. I believe I receive when I pray. I believe that what I say is done, having faith in God. He always comes through when I meet this condition of believing I receive, even though I may not see any change or feel any different at the moment. I have stood in faith in this manner and received financial breakthrough as a result. I have prayed and believed I received when it came to the healing of my body at different times and experienced God's healing power because I took Him at His Word.

Faith is believing you receive when you pray. This is the faith principle for answered prayer. Perhaps you have been praying and praying and praying about the same thing and experiencing little results. Change your approach. Lift your voice and your hands and begin praising and thanking God for answering your prayer as if you already received that answer. Give Him glory for it before you see or feel anything. Count it done and glorify Him as if He has heard and has responded. In other words, you have prayed. Now believe that you receive. Praying in this manner pleases God. And when the Father is pleased, He rewards those who diligently seek Him!

Work Sheet

What pleases God?

_____

Can we please God without believing Him?

_____

How does faith come?

_____
_____

How is faith shown in regards to prayer?

_____
_____
_____

To the world, 'seeing is believing.' In the kingdom of God, 'believing is seeing.' Explain the difference.

_____
_____
_____
_____
_____

Specific Kinds Of Prayer

Chapter Seven
GIVING GOD GLORY

Romans 15:4
4 For whatsoever things were written aforetime were written for our learning, that we through patience and comfort of the scriptures might have hope.

While we are now living under a New Covenant filled with better, greater and advantageous promises – guaranteed because of the precious blood of Christ and our great, faithful and only High Priest Himself – it is noteworthy to understand that there is much we can learn from the Old Covenant and those who lived under it. Indeed, the Apostle Paul constantly quoted from it in his messages inspired by the Spirit of God and even told us that there are things in that covenant (testament) which serve as examples for how God views some things. He points out things we can learn about God's ways – things which please Him and things which don't please Him.

We can also learn from the examples of those who believed God and had faith in His power and ability to deliver in times of danger and trouble. While some may want to argue this point, please remember that all of those spoken of in that great chapter on faith – Hebrews chapter eleven – were people from the Old Covenant who learned to believe God regardless of and above what they may have presently seen or felt. This statement is verified easily if you examine the lives of men of faith like Daniel, Abraham and Enoch. They dared to believe God and what He told them – whether by His Spirit, or by His revealed promises in His covenant – and God came through for them, showing Himself merciful and faithful. Faith pleases Him and when He is pleased, He will do the miraculous.

What is faith? While some may determine to give complicated answers or answers which are infused with theological or philosophical determinations, suffice it to say that faith is simply believing God based upon what He reveals. Faith is trusting God based upon His promises. Faith is relying on God to keep His Word, knowing that He will and acting like His Word is true.

Faith is standing so firm upon the Word that one refuses to be moved by what he or she feels or sees, knowing that things which are seen are subject to change and to be brought into conformity to what God has revealed. In other words, faith – in its simplest definition – means to believe God. We believe Him based upon knowledge – based upon His

Word. And because we believe Him, we act upon His Word. We walk in obedience to Him for we trust Him.

In this chapter, we shall examine two stories of men who believed God and how they gave glory and praise to God because they believed Him, even when circumstances and situations seemed contrary to what God said. If we learn to give God glory in advance, believing we receive when we pray, the results we receive in prayer will be marvelous and astound those around us. God is ever ready to answer our prayers. He wants to! This is one reason why He gave us access into His Presence. He wanted us to walk with Him, know Him and trust Him. However, He has established the principle of faith as the way to move His Hand in our favor. He is waiting on us to believe Him!

Hebrews 11:6
6 But without faith it is impossible to please him: for he that cometh to God must believe that he is, and that he is a rewarder of them that diligently seek him.

The stories we will look at are not new. They may prove very familiar to you. However, do not pass over them quickly because you think that you know them. We are looking to see how believing God and giving Him glory in advance – in spite of what seemed evident – resulted in the miraculous power of Almighty God moving in tremendous fashion. God is the same God now that He was then. He does not change. If we learn to praise, thank and glorify His Name before we see answers to our prayers, like our prayers are already answered, Jesus Himself guarantees that what we are giving God glory for shall be done. He promised it. The question is, *"Do we believe Him?"*

King Jehoshaphat's Faith Move

It was an interesting time in Judah. The kingdom had already been divided because of King Solomon's sin against Jehovah. The 10 tribes of the Northern kingdom of Israel had an evil king, King Ahab, and evil king. And the Southern kingdom of Judah had its own king, a godly man, named Jehoshaphat.

It was at this time when three nations – the children of Ammon, Moab and Mount Seir – decided to band together and come against Judah. They formed a mighty alliance, one that concerned King Jehoshaphat and his people. There was simply no way that Judah could defeat them, unless they received help. Being a man who served the Lord with a pure heart, the king made a very wise decision. He called a fast and a time of prayer for the entire Nation of Judah. They came together to ask help of the Lord. This is one of the reasons for prayer – that we may ask help of the Lord. We are told to come boldly to the throne of grace to find help in time of need. (See Hebrews 4:16)

It is interesting and noteworthy to examine Jehoshaphat's prayer on behalf of the people of

Judah. The very first thing he did was to acknowledge God and glorify Him for Who He was. In other words, he began the prayer with worship of the greatness of God. This is important, because He gave God His rightful place. He did not exalt the problem above his God. He did not deny there was an issue, however, he did not magnify it above his God. He gave God glory first by acknowledging God for Who He was. And Who He was, He still is, for He does not change. We should follow his example when we pray.

Don't begin your prayer talking about the issue and how bad things are. God is Greater! Therefore, begin the prayer by acknowledging Him for Who He is and giving Him glory.

2Chronicles 20: 5-6
5 And Jehoshaphat stood in the congregation of Judah and Jerusalem, in the house of the LORD, before the new court,
6 And said, O LORD God of our fathers, art not thou God in heaven? and rulest not thou over all the kingdoms of the heathen? and in thine hand is there not power and might, so that none is able to withstand thee?

Next, he reminded God of what He had done in the past. This is powerful! By calling to remembrance what God already did, it inspires faith to believe Him to do even more. Look at what he said to the Lord concerning past exploits.

2Chronicles 20:7
7 Art not thou our God, who didst drive out the inhabitants of this land before thy people Israel, and gavest it to the seed of Abraham thy friend for ever?

What did Jehoshaphat do here? He gave God glory by acknowledging what God did. So first, He gave God glory for Who He was and is, and now He says, *"God, You drove the inhabitants of the land out before Your people. You gave this land to us."* What powerful words!

It is good for us to do this as well. When we pray, we should give God glory for things He has done for us in the past. Give Him glory for healing your body. Give Him glory for meeting your needs. Give Him glory for giving you peace at a time when everything around you was in turmoil. Give Him glory for healing your emotions, or for restoring some relationship that was going wrong. Give Him glory for miracles you have experienced or seen Him do. Go to the Word and give Him glory for things He has done in the Word. Give Him glory most of all for loving you so much that He gave His only begotten Son, so that you would not perish, but have everlasting life. Give God glory for what He has already done for you!

Third, King Jehoshaphat reminded God of His Word! He brought the promises of God before Him. Listen, this is key to receiving answers to prayer. As we said in a previous chapter, we must have God's

Word abiding within us to be assured of an answer to prayer. Jesus said we must abide in Him and His Words must abide in us. We must search God's Word on the issue – for whatever we are dealing with. (Read John 15:7) Here is what Jehoshaphat said:

2Chronicles 20: 7-9
7 Art not thou our God, who didst drive out the inhabitants of this land before thy people Israel, and gavest it to the seed of Abraham thy friend for ever?
8 And they dwelt therein, and have built thee a sanctuary therein for thy name, saying,
9 If, when evil cometh upon us, as the sword, judgment, or pestilence, or famine, we stand before this house, and in thy presence, (for thy name is in this house,) and cry unto thee in our affliction, then thou wilt hear and help.

He said in essence, *"God, You said if we ever have a problem, all we have to do is cry to you as we stand before Your house."* They bought God's Word back to Him. They put Him in remembrance of His Word. Isaiah spoke of this as well.

Isaiah 43:26
26 Put me in remembrance: let us plead together: declare thou, that thou mayest be justified.

If you desire to see answers to prayer, follow this principle. Bring God's Word back to Him. He has promised that His Word shall not return to Him void, but it shall accomplish what He pleases and shall prosper in the thing whereunto He sends it. (See Isaiah 55:11). Here's my question? God said that His Word would not return to Him void. Who returns the Word back to Him? We do through prayer!

Next, King Jehoshaphat tells God the problem. He finally gets to the issue, after acknowledging God's greatness and reminding God of His Word. Here is what he said:

2Chronicles 20:10-11
10 And now, behold, the children of Ammon and Moab and mount Seir, whom thou wouldest not let Israel invade, when they came out of the land of Egypt, but they turned from them, and destroyed them not;
11 Behold, I say, how they reward us, to come to cast us out of thy possession, which thou hast given us to inherit.

That was the problem they were facing. These armies had come against them. They were picking a fight with them – an unwarranted fight. He then tells God what he wanted Him to do, humbling himself (and his people) before the Lord by letting Him know that they were not able to defeat these armies by themselves. They needed God! Oh, what a sacred, precious and marvelous place to arrive at in truth. When we acknowledge our utter dependence and need for God, and we cry out to Him for help, He will move on our behalf. They said those wonderful words: **"O our God, wilt thou not judge them? for we have no might against this great company that** cometh against us; neither know we what to do: but our eyes are upon thee." 2Chronicles 20:12.

What a powerful prayer!

Was God pleased with their requests? Of course, He was. He moved so mightily that He turned each of those evil armies against each other. They literally killed each other. Judah did not even have to fight. They walked into that camp and all of those who had come against them were dead. Judah spent three days collecting the jewels and the stuff those people had there – three days! What an awesome thing!

Now, this was the end of the story. However, we must retrace our steps to see what actually happened. When King Jehoshaphat finished praying, the Spirit of God came upon a Levite named Jahaziel. He spoke prophetically and God told the king and the people of Judah not to be afraid. He told them that they would not need to fight in this battle. He said that this was His battle and He would fight for them. Wow! We are now getting to the central point of the story. What was Jehoshaphat's response to what God said? God told them, **"for the battle is not yours, but God's."** God told them, **"Ye shall not need to fight in this battle:"** What was the proper response? Remember beloved, God loves to be believed. He loves when we operate by faith. How did Jehoshaphat and the children of Judah show their faith in God's rhema word to them? First, they bowed before the Lord, and began to worship Him. They had heard from God. They had a word from God.

God assured them that He was fighting this battle for them. They would not need to fight. How does one respond to such transcending promises? They worshipped. This showed their faith!

2Chronicles 20:18
18 And Jehoshaphat bowed his head with his face to the ground: and all Judah and the inhabitants of Jerusalem fell before the LORD, worshipping the LORD.

They worshipped! Glory to God! Then they began to praise God. They were not quiet about it either. They praised Him aloud.

2Chronicles 20:19
19 And the Levites, of the children of the Kohathites, and of the children of the Korhites, stood up to praise the LORD God of Israel with a loud voice on high.

What a demonstration of faith!

The enemy was still surrounding their city. They were still there. They could be seen. Yet, Judah knew what God had said. They would not need to fight in this battle. It was not their battle. It was His. Oh, they worshipped and praised Him. Their attention was not on their enemies. Their attention was no longer on what they were facing. They were not being moved anymore by what they saw physically. Yes, the enemies were still there. But, God had spoken. To them, that settled the matter. Is it this way with us? Is His Word enough for us?

Then they took another step of faith. After worship and praise, instead of King Jehoshaphat placing the army in front – knowing that God had already said they would not need to fight in this battle – he placed the praisers in the front. He placed people in front to continually give God praise and glory as if the battle was already won and they were already the victors. As far as he was concerned, it was a done deal. Here is how the scriptures says it:

2Chronicles 20: 20-21
20 And they rose early in the morning, and went forth into the wilderness of Tekoa: and as they went forth, Jehoshaphat stood and said, Hear me, O Judah, and ye inhabitants of Jerusalem; Believe in the LORD your God, so shall ye be established; believe his prophets, so shall ye prosper.
21 And when he had consulted with the people, he appointed singers unto the LORD, and that should praise the beauty of holiness, as they went out before the army, and to say, Praise the LORD; for his mercy endureth for ever.

Wow! There is much we can learn here. However, what I want to point out is that they literally acted as though their prayers had been heard and their prayers had been answered. They gave God praise, glory and thanksgiving for the victory before they ever saw anything. They acted as though it was done. And God came through for them BIG-TIME!

2Chronicles 20: 22-24
22 And when they began to sing and to praise, the LORD set ambushments against the children of Ammon, Moab, and mount Seir, which were come against Judah; and they were smitten.
23 For the children of Ammon and Moab stood up against the inhabitants of mount Seir, utterly to slay and destroy them: and when they had made an end of the inhabitants of Seir, every one helped to destroy another.
24 And when Judah came toward the watch tower in the wilderness, they looked unto the multitude, and, behold, they were dead bodies fallen to the earth, and none escaped.

Pay close attention to those first nine words in verse twenty-two carefully!

It says, **"And when they began to sing and to praise."** These words are very important. God had given His Word. They had prayed and He had spoken. He told them that they would not need to fight in this battle. He had told them that this battle was not theirs, but His. Now, He was waiting on them to show they believed Him. It was when they began to sing and praise Him (before they ever saw the victory) that God moved by His power, influencing the enemies to destroy each other. They showed God they believed Him. They worshipped and glorified, and thanked Him before they saw anything. They did it as if it was already done. When they took this position of faith, God moved by His power, and the rest is history. Likewise, when we practice praising and thanking God in advance, giving Him glory as if our prayers have been heard and answered because we have prayed according to His Word – WATCH OUT! He will move on our behalf in ways that will astound the world!

Abraham's Faith Move

Upon hearing a word directly from Jehovah Himself, Abram and his wife left Ur of the Chaldees, not knowing where he was going. Although God told him to leave his father's house, he did take his father, Terah with him. He also took his nephew, Lot.

This was a journey of faith and Abram was so sure that He had heard from the Creator Himself that he was ready and willing to move forward with what Jehovah had spoken. He came to the land of Canaan and journeyed through and in the land for years. God had also given him a precious promise. He had told him that if he would obey Him, that He would bless him and make his name great and that He would give him a seed who would cause all nations upon the face of the earth to be blessed. There was just one problem – not a problem for El Shaddai! Abraham's wife was barren. She could not have children in the natural. Nevertheless, Almighty God had spoken and Abram believed God. Now how was God going to bring this word to pass? Abram did not know. As a matter of fact, when Sarah told Abram that it might be that God wanted him to have seed through their maid, Hagah, Abram went for it. Through that union – unapproved of God – they had Ishmael. However, this was not what God wanted. This was not the promised seed, not even the natural promised seed. Abram did believe God would give him seed. He just did not think it would come through Sarah apparently. She was barren. But God specializes in the impossible. He loves to show Himself strong on behalf of those who are loyal to Him and choose to believe Him above what they may see or feel. He is moved by our faith in what He promises. Faith pleases God! So, God waited for it to actually be impossible in the natural for Abram or Sarah to have a child. He waited until they were old – really old.

While we are not doing a full study on the life of Abraham here, it is worth knowing that he did have his doubts. He could not see how what God had spoken would become a reality. However, God needed him to be in agreement with Him, so He changed his name from Abram to Abraham – which means, 'the father of a great multitude.' So, every time someone called his name, they were saying, 'father of a great multitude.' Wow! On one hand this was a great faith-builder, for it was a confession and affirmation of that which the Lord God had promised. On the other hand, it might have also produced some unwanted criticism and persecution, for Abraham was calling forth those things which were not (presently) as though they were. This was faith in action. He was saying what God had declared him to be. He was saying what God said about him.

He was agreeing with God. Therefore, he walked with God! (See Amos 3:3)

Romans 4: 16 -18
16 Therefore it is of faith, that it might be by grace; to the end the promise might be sure to all the seed; not to that only which is of the law, but to that also which is of the faith of Abraham; who is the father of us all,
17 (As it is written, I have made thee a father of many nations,) before him whom he believed, even God, who quickeneth the dead, and calleth those things which be not as though they were.
18 Who against hope believed in hope, that he might become the father of many nations, according to that which was spoken, So shall thy seed be.

Abraham, like God, called those things which were not (yet manifested) as though they were. He was not lying. He was saying what God said about him! If we will dare to say what God says about us, it shall become a manifested reality in our lives, just like what God said regarding Abraham became a manifested reality. That reality is still manifesting to this day, for we are also Abraham's seed and heirs according to that which God had promised. (Read Galatians 3:29)

We are looking at principles of faith that Abraham practiced that we may gain knowledge and wisdom that will ensure that we receive answers to our prayers. One of the things we can learn right away is that Abraham had God's Word regarding what he was believing for. God had spoken to him. He had God's Word for it. Take note again that our Lord Jesus Christ said God's Words (which are His promises) must be abiding within us if we desire to see our prayers answered. God's written Word is filled with His promises to us. They belong to us now in Christ Jesus. We have His Word, just as Abraham had His Word many centuries ago. Glory to God!

The second thing we can see in Abraham's journey of faith is that we must practice keeping God's Word in our mouths. Let us consider this in the light of what Jesus said regarding the mountain moving prayer of faith. We are speaking of calling things which be not as though they were or are. We must practice speaking in line with God. We cannot pray, then speak continually contrary to what we have prayed, expecting God to answer our prayers. Faith says what God says. Faith disciplines the tongue to speak in line with God. Here is that wonderful promise of Jesus again.

Mark 11:24
24 Therefore I say unto you, What things soever ye desire, when ye pray, believe that ye receive them, and ye shall have them.

Consider this powerful and life-changing promise in the light of Abraham's life of faith!

Abraham was given a promise of God that he would have seed through whom all nations of the earth would be blessed. (The reason we are also Abraham's seed in God's Eyes is because the promised seed was Christ. Yes, in the natural, God was speaking of Isaac. However, He was actually speaking of the One Who would come through Isaac's line to redeem humanity – the Lord Jesus Christ, the Son of Abraham. (See Matthew 1:1)

God needed Abraham to speak in line with Him, to be in agreement with Him. He needed Abraham to walk by faith, not by sight, for faith pleases God. So, Abraham began speaking of himself as the father of a great multitude, or the father of many nations before Isaac was even an embryo in Sarah's womb. God was faithful and brought His Word to pass even though in the natural it could not happen. Yet, it did happen!

Abraham believed God and God give him and Sarah a son. From that son came Jacob through whom came the twelve sons of Israel. From the twelve sons came the twelve tribes, and from the twelve tribes came the Nation of Israel. Glory to God!

How does this correspond with the promise the Master gave in Mark chapter eleven, verse twenty-four? We are to believe we receive what we pray for when we pray – not when we see or feel it. We are to believe it is ours the moment we ask for it. We are to believe it is granted to us as soon as we ask for it. And our confession from that moment on should show that we believe we receive when we prayed.

Therefore, when we pray for healing, we are to begin confessing and affirming that we believe we are healed – not continue asking God to heal us as though He did not hear us the first time. When we ask Him to meet a need, we are to speak as though it is done, thanking God in advance for what we may not yet see or what may not yet have manifested. It is as we choose to believe God based upon the promise of Jesus Christ Himself that Heaven goes to work on our behalf. It is a faith walk!

The third thing that we need to take note of is that the Bible says Abraham was strong in faith, giving glory to God, even before he and Sarah ever had their son, Isaac.

Romans 4: 19-21
19 And being not weak in faith, he considered not his own body now dead, when he was about an hundred years old, neither yet the deadness of Sara's womb:
20 He staggered not at the promise of God through unbelief; but was strong in faith, giving glory to God;
21 And being fully persuaded that, what he had promised, he was able also to perform.

He did not care how it appeared. He knew what God had said, believed what God had said and said what God had said. He did not concern himself with how God was going to do it. He simply believed He was able to, powerful enough, and more than enough to do as He had said. He became fully persuaded.

God persuaded him through His Word. How did Abraham become strong in faith? If we discover the answer to this, we can also become strong in our faith in God and see wonderful, continuous, miraculous answers to our prayers. God is not a respector of persons. He is a respector of faith. *He moves mightily on our behalf when we choose to believe Him!* How did Abraham become strong in faith? He was not always that way. The situation with Hagar and Ishmael proved that. Abraham grew in faith. We already saw that he brought his words in line with what God had said about him. God saw to that by having him change his name. But was there something else that he did. YES! Notice this powerful scripture again.

Romans 4: 20-21
20 He staggered not at the promise of God through unbelief; but was strong in faith, giving glory to God;
21 And being fully persuaded that, what he had promised, he was able also to perform.

Abraham practiced worshipping and giving God glory, calling things which were not yet manifested as though they were. He worshipped and gave God glory for making him the father of a great multitude, even before Isaac was born. He gave God glory in advance as though it was done. It is brought out beautifully in the **Amplified Bible Classic Edition.** I would encourage you to meditate for a few moments upon these words. They are life-transforming and will unveil a precious truth concerning the faith life. It may be the reason so many believers may not be experiencing answers to their prayer.

Romans 4: 20-21 (AMPC)
20 No unbelief or distrust made him waver (doubtingly question) concerning the promise of God, but he grew strong and was empowered by faith as he gave praise and glory to God,
21 Fully satisfied and assured that God was able and mighty to keep His word and to do what He had promised.

This is powerful!

Abraham grew strong in faith. He was empowered by faith. As he gave praise and glory to God, knowing that God would keep His Word to him. He worshipped God in advance as though it was already done. He grew in faith through private worship. He gave God praise and glory. Jesus said that we are to believe we receive what we ask for when we pray. And how are we to show God that we believe we receive when we pray? We are to praise, thank and give Him glory in advance, as though what we ask is granted from our wonderful Heavenly Father. If we practice doing this, we shall grow in faith and be empowered through faith. We shall be pleasing to our Father and He shall move mightily on our behalf!

In both of these cases that we have examined from God's Word, the people of God worshipped, praised and thanked God in advance, even before they saw or experienced the miracle they were believing God for. Both King Jehoshaphat and Abraham gave God praise and glory in advance as though what God had said was a done deal. And in both cases, their faith resulted in the mighty power of God moving in tremendous ways, bringing forth the miraculous as only God can do. These serve as examples to us of what would happen if we practice giving God glory and praise in advance as though we already have what we have asked Him for in prayer. Jesus said, **"Therefore I say unto you, What things soever ye desire, when ye pray, believe that ye receive them, and ye shall have them."**

Giving God glory, thanks and worship in advance shows that we believe we receive!

Work Sheet

How did Abraham become strong in faith?

When are we to give God glory and thanksgiving in faith, before we receive what we have prayed for or after we see or feel it?

Is believing one receives before one sees lying? Please explain your answer.

What does it mean to give God glory?

Chapter Eight
FAITH & PATIENCE

If we are truly going to enjoy answers to prayer, we will have to practice exercising patience. God's answers to our request may not manifest right away, the moment that we ask.

Much of the time, we may not immediately see or feel what we have prayed for. God's Word teaches that being steadfast and consistent is vital to receiving from Him. Consider for an example what we are told in the Book of James.

James 1: 5-8
2 My brethren, count it all joy when ye fall into divers temptations;
3 Knowing this, that the trying of your faith worketh patience.
4 But let patience have her perfect work, that ye may be perfect and entire, wanting nothing.
5 If any of you lack wisdom, let him ask of God, that giveth to all men liberally, and upbraideth not; and it shall be given him.

**6 But let him ask in faith, nothing wavering. For he that wavereth is like a wave of the sea driven with the wind and tossed.
7 For let not that man think that he shall receive any thing of the Lord.
8 A double minded man is unstable in all his ways.**

What Is Patience

We must consider what real patience is according to the scriptures and in the light of faith and patience. First, let us look at what the Greek word for patience means.

Patience come from the **Greek** word *Hypomonē*. According to the **James Strong's Exhaustive Concordance,** it means *steadfastness, constancy and endurance. In the N. T. the characteristic of a man who is unswerved from his deliberate purpose and his loyalty to faith and piety by even the greatest trials and sufferings.*

To be steadfast means to be firmly fixed in place. It speaks of being consistent. Patience is literally holding fast to one's belief, holding fast to the Word of God, until what one is believing God for is manifested. Patience is not being restless or wishful, or watching and wondering if God heard you and if He is really going to come through for you this time. Patience, in prayer, describes the person who is consistently showing that he or she believes God has heard their prayer and that they believe they receive. This is demonstrated in how they behave, the words they continually say, and through praise and thanksgiving. It is not worrying and fretting until one sees the answer. It is literally resting in the promise of God until it is manifested – going about one's day worshipping and thanking God for hearing our prayer, acting like it is a done deal. Faith and patience operate together. While faith stands upon the precious promises of God, patience keeps us standing there.

We are told here that we can ask God for wisdom – which in the context refers to asking for His insight, plan, and help to handle whatever test, trial or temptation we may be facing. However, we can also ask for His wisdom in our marriages, finances, schooling, choosing of friendships, handling of issues that we face, and our occupations as well. His wisdom will teach us how to be better parents, handle money better and deal with situations and circumstances in ways which cause us to excel at whatever we place our hands to. We are given the guarantee that if we ask Him for His wisdom, He will grant it. Here is The Message Bible's rendering of verse five.

James 1:5 (MSG)
If you don't know what you're doing, pray to the Father. He loves to help. You'll get his help, and won't be condescended to when you ask for it.

Isn't that wonderful! God says if we ask for His wisdom when facing a challenge, He will grant it. We will receive His help. However, there is a requirement. We must ask in faith. Again, faith moves the hand of God on our behalf and in our situations, because it is impossible to bring Him pleasure without it. He longs to be believed. So, we must ask believing we will receive when we pray. And once we ask for His wisdom in a situation, we must believe that it is granted to us, praising and thanking Him for it. This is where patience must kick in. We must now be consistent in giving praise and thanks for His wisdom knowing and believing – trusting – that we have it, that He has answered our requests. We must not permit ourselves to waver in this regard. We must count it done and act like it's done, giving glory to God in advance.

Wavering means that we are not exercising patience. It shows a lack of faith on our part, for we are still looking at the condition of things as they may still appear, instead of through the eyes of faith. God says very clearly that the person who wavers (or doubts) is like the waves of the sea, driven with the wind and tossed. In other words, this describes the person who is one moment saying, *"I believe God heard and answered my prayer,"* but when things don't seem to be changing right away or they don't seem to know what to do or how to handle the challenge quickly enough, they say, *"I don't know what to do. I don't know how to handle this. I wonder if God answered my prayer."* They are moved by the circumstances instead of by faith in God's Word. Beloved, we can trust God. We can believe Him. We do not have to doubt Him. He says to ask and that He will grant it. We can take Him at His Word for He cannot lie.

God says that the person who wavers or doubts **WILL NOT** receive anything of the Lord. Wow! **WILL NOT!** So, if we want to be assured of answers to our prayers, we must ask in faith, believing that when we pray, He has answered. Then we must be patient, giving Him thanks and praise as though we already have what we have prayed for until manifestation occurs. Thank Him daily. Be consistent in this. Your faith will grow and soon you will really believe you have what you have requested from the Father. And when you arrive at this place, your answer will manifest perhaps sooner than you even thought it would.

Work Sheet

Walking by faith requires patience. Explain this statement.

_____
_____
_____
_____

What is Bible patience? Please explain what it is and what it is not.

_____
_____
_____

When we truly believe God, what are we constantly doing until the answer to our prayer is manifested?

_____
_____

What does it mean to be consistent in faith?

_____
_____
_____
_____

Chapter Nine
THE OBSTACLE OF UN-FORGIVENESS

Perhaps the greatest hindrance to answered prayer – other than ignorance of God's will in a matter – is the obstacle of an unforgiving heart.

We all love those powerful and life-changing words from the lips of the Master as He declared that we can speak to our mountains, and if we believe, they would be thrown into the sea. We love what He said regarding prayer, that we can pray and believe we receive when we pray, and what we ask for shall be done. Those are wonderful words, glorious words, transforming words of victory.

However, the Lord did not finish teaching yet. Let's look at what He said in the gospel of Mark chapter eleven again. However, this time, we shall not stop at verse twenty-four. We shall listen to the rest of what He said.

Mark 11: 22-26
22 And Jesus answering saith unto them, Have faith in God.
23 For verily I say unto you, That whosoever shall say unto this mountain, Be thou removed, and be thou cast into the sea; and shall not doubt in his heart, but shall believe that those things which he saith shall come to pass; he shall have whatsoever he saith.
24 Therefore I say unto you, What things soever ye desire, when ye pray, believe that ye receive them, and ye shall have them.
25 And when ye stand praying, forgive, if ye have ought against any: that your Father also which is in heaven may forgive you your trespasses.
26 But if ye do not forgive, neither will your Father which is in heaven forgive your trespasses.

What a loaded statement! Jesus gave us the principles of the Kingdom here. He revealed how to walk by faith and receive answers to prayer. And included in those principles, He gave us one of the main things which can hinder or block our progress in the faith life. Some people may wish that He had left that part out. After all, He is speaking of forgiving those who may have wronged us in any way.

Forgive

Many believers are walking around with bitter hearts, filled with malice and strife. Yet, they constantly pray as though their dealing with their fellowman have nothing to do with their relationship with God. This is a delusion! We cannot walk with God holding unforgiveness against people for things they may have said or done that offended us. We will have to practice forgiving those who wrong us if we want our prayers answered. Now while some may think that this may have to be some long drawn out process that can only happen with time, according to Jesus, forgiving others does not have to take long.

Notice carefully that Jesus said, ***"When ye stand praying, forgive, if ye have ought against any:"*** He said at the same moment that you are praying, forgive. This means we can choose to forgive those who may have offended us right away. It does not have to take years or months or even days. It can take just a minute, just a second. It takes a decision. Now notice that I did not say, *"It takes a feeling."* I said, *"It takes a decision."* There is a huge difference between the two. While the feelings of forgiveness may take some time, the decision to forgive can take a moment.

Forgiveness Is Not A Feeling

The Lord Jesus Christ said that as we stand praying – the same time while we are praying – we are to forgive if we have anything against anyone.

According to the Master, it does not have to be a long process. It can happen instantly, as we pray. Does the Lord not understand that forgiveness is a process which has to take weeks of counselling, months of therapy and years of working things out? Does He not know that we cannot forgive just like that? Perhaps we are the ones who do not understand the difference between pain and forgiveness.

Offense

Consider for a moment what an offense is!

According to **Webster's Online Dictionary 1828 Edition**, the word *offense* means the following:

. *something that outrages the moral or physical senses.*

. *the act of displeasing or affronting.*

. *the state of being insulted or morally outraged.*

In plain words, offense happens when someone (whether intentionally or unintentionally) says or does something to a person or against a person which hurts them – either emotionally or physically or both. Offense can and does hurt.

Now it is also wise to consider the fact that while offenses may come, one can choose not be become offended. There is a place in God where this is truly attainable. Many in Christendom through the years have experienced persecution, tribulation and sufferings at the hands of merciless rulers and people, yet they walked in such a tremendous depth of the love and compassion of Christ that they refused to be offended at their opponents. Instead, they mercifully prayed that the Lord would forgive them and not lay their evil deeds to their charge. Can this be true for us today? Of course it can. We serve the same Jesus. And He has shed abroad His love in our hearts just as He did those believers who experienced such a fate. We simply have to learn to trust and walk with our God closely, refusing to be moved by our feelings, until His love swallows us up from within and consumes us. Jesus said the following words; **"It is impossible but that offences will come: but woe unto him, through whom they come!"** (See Luke 17:1)

Offenses will come!

The Greek word for offense here is the word *skandalon.* According to the **James Strong's Exhaustive Concordance,** it means a *trap stick or a snare.* It speaks of *any impediment placed in the way and causing one to stumble or fall, (a stumbling block, occasion of stumbling).*

There is no amount of prayer, no amount of fasting that will stop offenses from coming. Someone somewhere will not like you for some reason, or will decide to hurt you – whether with words or actions – just because they think they can. Some family member may decide to push you and get on your last nerve. Some seeming best friend may decide to betray a sacred trust and tell some secret that you hoped would stay between you and them. Some evil boss may say cruel things against you, or someone on your job may decide to lie on you because they desire your position. Some minister may not like your ministry because it is different, and decide to come against you for no apparent reason other than jealousy. Some church member may decide to spread untrue and unfounded rumors about you. Offenses will come – not may come – will come. Jesus said so!

With that offense may come shame, hurt and pain. However, we can determine not to become offended or not to stay offended. We can forgive! Prayers can be blocked if we allow the seed of unforgiveness to take root in our hearts and grow up into a tree of bitterness and iniquity. Here is what the Word says:

Psalms 66:18
18 If I regard iniquity in my heart, the Lord will not hear me:

This is why Jesus said that we are to forgive when we stand praying. We must guard our hearts from bitterness, which leads to anger and wrath. It is not a matter of justifying the person who may have wronged us or saying that they were right with what they may have said or done. A lot of times what they said or did was indeed wrong. Forgiving them has more to do with three things.

> 1. *Obeying the Lord, realizing that we also need forgiveness at times. God is so good to us that He forgives us when we confess we have missed the mark.* Do we actually deserve His

forgiveness and mercy? No, we do not! Nevertheless, He does so because He loves us. He desires that we follow His example.

2. *Forgiving others clears the way for our prayers to be heard and therefore answered.* It releases the stress, anxiety and potential for becoming bitter from our hearts. It frees us to walk with our God – for He is Love. We are able to approach His Throne of grace and make our requests known without hindrance!

3. *Forgiving others may keep the way clear that we can in some way present or reveal Jesus to those who may have wronged us.* This is vital, for it may lead to their salvation or their deliverance from the enemy at some point. There is so much that can be said in this regard. By walking in love and forgiveness we can pray for those who may have wronged us – binding the real enemy from them and loosing them from his strongholds. Jesus said we are to pray for our enemies, referring to people the devil may influence to do us wrong. They may be blinded to the fact that he is using them. They may not even know what they are doing. Then again, they may know. Nevertheless, we are told to forgive them, and this places us in a position to be used by the Spirit of God in intercession for them! (Read Matthew 18: 15-35 & Matthew 5: 43-45)

What It Means To Forgive

We must differentiate between true forgiveness and "feelings" of unforgiveness!

Many people believe that they would be lying if they decide to obey the Lord Jesus and forgive those who offend them – whether by word or deed – while feelings of anger, wrath or hostility remain. This is a weapon the enemy uses to hold God's people in bondage. We are not our feelings. We are not our emotions. We have emotions, but how we feel at any given time should not determine what we choose to do or not to do. Our feelings constantly change. And while we have feelings, we are never to govern our affairs based upon our feelings – especially if they oppose the Word and will of the Father.

When it comes to this area of forgiveness, this is more of a decision to obey than a feeling to consider. The word "forgive" in Mark chapter eleven, verses twenty-five and twenty-six comes from the **Greek** word ***aphiēmi.*** According to the **James Strong's Exhaustive Concordance**, it means *to send forth.* It means *to lay aside, leave alone or to let go.* What is interesting is that it never means "to feel like letting go, or to feel like laying the matter aside." Feelings are not even considered here. Why is this the case? Because forgiveness has to do with the will more than it has to do with the emotions. What does it mean to forgive? It means to let the person go who may have wronged you. Just as the Father God dropped the charges against us when we came to

Jesus, He now wants us to drop the charges against those who may have hurt us through words or deeds. And He has placed His love within our hearts giving us the ability to do this regardless of how we may feel.

Romans 5:5
5And hope maketh not ashamed; because the love of God is shed abroad in our hearts by the Holy Ghost which is given unto us.

We have the love of God on the inside of us, giving us the ability to love like God loves and to forgive, even as God for Christ's sake, has forgiven us!

We must practice yielding to His love within us and learn to let things go that people may have said or done against us – the wrongs we have suffered. Learn to forgive by faith, because Jesus said we can. And remember that He said we are to forgive others as we stand praying. This means that we can forgive people right away, regardless of how we feel at the moment. *Remember, forgiveness is not a feeling. It is a decision!*

If we determine to forgive because the Master said we are to do so, the time may come when we have those feelings of forgiveness and sense the compassion of Christ rising up within us for those who may have wronged us. But do not let your feelings master and control you. You control them! How do you do this? You simply say, ***"Father, in obedience to Your Word, I choose to forgive this*** *person – or these people – for the wrong they have done to me. I choose to let them go now, and I also ask dear Father that You forgive me for holding something in my heart against them, in Jesus Name. Now Father, forgive them also for what they did, in Jesus Name. I pray Your blessings upon them and that You would help them and favor them in Jesus Name. Thank You Father for hearing my prayers, for I pray in Jesus Name. Amen!"*

Now the enemy will whisper in your ear, *"You did not really forgive them. Look at how you feel. Do you feel like you forgive them? You are lying. You feel like getting even, right? You just lied to God."* And your feelings may be in agreement with those thoughts. Answer him back by saying, *"I choose to forgive, not by feelings, but by choice in obedience to my wonderful Lord and Savior, Jesus Christ. I let the matter go. I choose to not hold a thing against this person in Jesus Name, and I don't care how I presently feel. My feelings do not rule me. I control my emotions, and I choose to forgive in Jesus Name."*

And from that moment on, just act like you have forgiven and walk free. If it was something evil that was done which strongly hurt or wounded your heart, emotions or even your body – ask the Healer of the broken hearted to heal and make you whole in Jesus Name. He will, for you qualify to receive from Him. You have obeyed Him by faith and chose to forgive. So He will honor your request. By the way, if you make a firm decision that you will also pray for the individual, you will find that compassion will rise up within you for them. You will realize that the real enemy behind what they did against you is the devil and that they yielded to him. Perhaps they were ignorant of it. Perhaps they need deliverance. Maybe they need you to bind the enemy on their behalf. Forgive and then pray for them whenever the Holy Spirit brings them to your heart and mind. Also, pray for them whenever the enemy attempts to stir up evil emotions against you through thoughts and evil imaginations. Praying for them will ease that tension and allow the love of God within you to flow more.

Forgiving others will free you and ensure that you are in position to receive answers to your prayers. So I encourage you not to hesitate or procrastinate in this regard. Do it and do it quickly. Jesus said to do it as you stand praying. Obey Him. He knows what it is to be treated worse than any other, and still choose to pray, **"Father forgive them, for they know not what they do."** (See Luke 23:46) He said to do it as we stand praying. This means it does not take long to make this decision. Let us do so, knowing that we need our connection with God to stay intact. We need answers to our prayers!

A Word Of Wisdom In This Regard

Now I do need to address a matter that many have wondered about. Someone may say, *"Suppose it was a best friend who betrayed a sacred trust. Am I supposed to trust that person with my private business again?"* The answer is "No." They have proven themselves unworthy of trust. So while you have forgiven, you cannot give them that opportunity to hurt you again in that manner. Nevertheless, you can still be friendly and not hostile towards them. Someone may say, *"Suppose the person sexually assaulted me. Am I to put myself in position for that to happen again?"* No, don't do that. As a matter of fact, because the law was broken, you should have reported the matter to the police. And no, you should not put yourself in the position for that to happen again. **Forgiving people does not mean acting without wisdom or without common sense.** While you choose to forgive, that does not mean you have to permit a person back into your life in any way who is not deserving of such a place. If they have proven that they cannot be trusted with your finances, do not give them that place in your life anymore. If they have proven they cannot be trusted with confidential information, do not give them any. If one cannot be trusted, or has broken a trust, you have the right to never allow them into that place in your life anymore, or until you are comfortable with them and have proven that they have changed!

Work Sheet

Name three major obstacles to answered prayer?

_____
_____
_____

What did the Lord Jesus say regarding prayer and forgiveness?

_____
_____
_____

Can believers expect answers to prayer while walking in un-forgiveness?

_____
_____

What does it mean to forgive?

_____
_____

Does one have to wait until he or she feels like forgiving before he or she chooses to forgive? Is forgiveness an emotion or a decision? Can one truly forgive regardless of how one feels?

_____
_____
_____

Specific Kinds Of Prayer

Chapter Ten
PRAYING FOR THE LOST

Up to this point, we have been gaining knowledge and wisdom of how to make our own petitions known, or how to pray for ourselves and receive answers from Heaven. Now let us look at praying for others!

The Bible teaches that we are to pray for others. We are to pray for the lost. We are to pray for the saints. We are to pray for those in ministry. We are to pray for leaders of nations and those in authority. We are to pray for the sick and for those under-going severe tests and trials. We are supposed to pray for others.

How are we supposed to pray for them? The scriptures give us great insight concerning this matter. If we pray according to God's Word, those who we pray for will receive favor, salvation, blessings, provision, healings, deliverance, strength, comfort, help, wisdom, instruction, understanding, knowledge, and guidance in various matters. Prayer works because God answers prayer!

Praying For The Lost

It is vitally important that we pray according to the will of God for others instead of praying to enforce our own will or desire upon them. If we keep our prayers for them in line with the things God has instructed us to pray for, we will see more results. We have already spoken concerning the prayer of salvation. But how do we pray for those who need Christ specifically? If we are praying for someone who does not know Christ, we can lead them in *"the sinner's prayer"* in chapter four. However, we are speaking of how to pray for them and present them to the Father. Many people need the Lord. Some of them are relatives, others may be acquaintances or friends. And others may be people we work with or perhaps our bosses. We may not even know some people personally who we are led to pray for. After all, we are always admonished to pray for the lost in foreign lands or to pray that as evangelists and missionaries go to carry the life-changing gospel of Christ, many would come to know the Lord in the pardon of their sins. How can we pray effectively for them? Here are some things to consider:

1. The unsaved are blinded by the enemy so that they cannot see the light of the gospel of the glory of Christ. We need to pray that the blindness be removed in Jesus Name so that

Specific Kinds Of Prayer

they can pay attention to and receive the good news. (See 2Corinthians 4:4)

2. Some people will not listen to certain people. We need to pray that God would lead the right person/people into the path of the person/people we are praying for. Some are anointed of God to reach people others may not be able to reach. We must trust the Lord to send whom He will, knowing that He knows who to send and who to send them to. He knows who can reach the one/ones we are praying for! (Read Matthew 9: 37-38)

3. While God anoints men and women, boys and girls to share the gospel with the lost, it is the Holy Spirit Himself Who actually draws us to Christ. We cannot come to Him unless the Father draws us. We should pray that the Spirit of God deals strongly with the hearts of the lost and give them no rest until they yield their lives to Jesus Christ. (Read John 6:37)

4. Some people need God to get their attention. We need the manifestation of the power of the Spirit of God in our midst, demonstrating Himself in miracles, signs and wonders to get the attention of the lost so that they will listen to the preaching of God's Word and realize how real God is. One miracle of God can get the attention of the masses for Christ. This is

Specific Kinds Of Prayer

proven throughout scripture and also in the ministries of men and women of God who spend much time in prayer asking for the Lord to manifest Himself through gifts of the Spirit. These precious endowments of the power of God are extremely necessary and will become even more needed as we continue to take the gospel of Christ to a sceptic, hostile and increasingly wicked generation. It will take the power of God to get their attention. We need to pray much for the manifestations of the Spirit to be in operation for the glory of the Risen Christ. (Read Hebrews 2:4)

Here is a prayer that we can pray for our lost loved ones:

Heavenly Father, we thank You for Your great love. We thank You so much for sending Your Son, the Lord Jesus Christ, to die for our sins, shedding His blood to wash our sins away. We thank You that You love us so much. Father, I bring _____ before You. He/she needs a relationship with You. I pray dear Father that You would send laborers across _____ path with the message of the gospel. I ask that You would draw them to Your Son, the Lord Jesus Christ, and that they would respond to His drawing. I break the bondage and blindness of the enemy from off of their minds in the authority of Jesus Name, and claim _____ full salvation and deliverance from the hands of the devil now in Jesus Name. And

Specific Kinds Of Prayer

Father, I thank You in advance for _____ salvation, and give You all praise, honor and glory for it, in Jesus precious Name. Amen!

We can pray that prayer for individuals we know. We can also word it to pray for other unsaved people we may not know. One of the things which is essential in prayer is that we need to learn dependence upon the Holy Spirit. While we give examples of how to pray for specific needs here, please do not neglect to listen for and heed the promptings of the Spirit to pray other specific things He may bring to your heart and mind. He knows what may be blocking individuals from yielding to Christ. And He knows how to teach us how to pray the person/persons past that obstacle which may be holding them back. These prayers are to give you a starting point in prayer. Let Him lead you on!

It is necessary to spend time praying in the Holy Spirit when praying for the lost as well. If we will yield our tongues to Him, He knows how to flow through us and pray exactly what needs to be prayed so that the Father can do all in His power to reach out to that person/persons being prayed for. The key here is to persist in prayer until you have that *"Divine Assurance"* that your prayer has been heard and answered. From that moment on, give God thanks and praise as though the work is done, regardless of what you may see. Once God confirms within your heart that it is done, you can rest in His faithfulness!

Work Sheet

Why should we pray for the unsaved?

_____
_____
_____

What should we pray for the unsaved?

_____
_____
_____

Why do we need to break the enemy's hold on the unsaved?

_____
_____
_____

Who truly draws the unbeliever to Christ?

_____

What is our role as believers and ministers of the Gospel in regard to the unsaved? Three answers required.

_____
_____
_____

Chapter Eleven
PRAYING IN THE SPIRIT

Ephesians 6:18
18 Praying always with all prayer and supplication in the Spirit, and watching thereunto with all perseverance and supplication for all saints;

It is vitally important that we practice praying the scriptures and that we pray in line with God's Word. It is also equally important that we learn the Mind and ways of the Holy Spirit in prayer!

Prayer is a Spirit to spirit connection with the Father. We connect with Him by yielding ourselves to the Holy Ghost in obedience. While we may know what the Word says, it is necessary to listen for the breath of the Spirit and pray according to His leading. This *'breath'* or flow of the Spirit takes time to learn. However, if we are willing to move with Him, it results in astounding answers to prayer. There are believers who have become so developed in this area that at the slightest breath, prompting or call of the Spirit, they get alone with the Father and yield themselves to Him. This leads into marvelous experiences with God as He flows through the believer to pray the perfect prayer that is needed in order to get the results that are needed.

How do we learn to pray in the Spirit – how to pray the Mind of Christ? First, we must comprehend our great need for the Holy Spirit. We need Him, period! Jesus sent Him to us and He has come with all of His power, all of His wisdom and all of His knowledge to help us, empower us and lead us into all truth. This includes truth regarding effective prayer and effective praying. He knows how to pray. We need to listen for Him. Again, Jesus said that He was sending us the **"Comforter."** The Holy Spirit is our Comforter. The Greek word for Comforter is the word *paraklētos.* According to the **James Strong's Exhaustive Concordance,** it literally means *an intercessor, consoler* or an *advocate.* The Amplified Bible Classic Edition gives the seven-fold meaning of the word. Here is the scripture in the Book of John as the Master speaks:

John 14:26 (AMPC)
26 But the Comforter (Counselor, Helper, Intercessor, Advocate, Strengthener, Standby), the Holy Spirit, Whom the Father will send in My name [in My place, to represent Me and act on My behalf], He will teach you all things. And He will cause you to recall (will remind you of, bring to your remembrance) everything I have told you.

Notice that the Holy Spirit, the One called alongside to help us, is – among other things – our Intercessor.

An intercessor is one who prays for another or who pleads another's case. How would you like for the Holy Spirit to do this for you? How would you like for Him to flow through you and do this for others? He longs and yearns to pray for us. He deeply desires to have us yield our tongues to Him so that He can pray the perfect prayer – the perfect will of God – for our lives, and for others. He will not force Himself upon us in this regard. We will have to yield to His leading – to His flow. How do we turn ourselves over to Him that He may pray for us through us? What does it mean to truly pray in the Spirit? Paul said, by the Holy Spirit that we are to – in addition to the other kinds of prayer – pray in the Spirit and persevere in prayer for fellow saints. What did he mean? He also said the following:

Romans 8: 26-28
26 Likewise the Spirit also helpeth our infirmities: for we know not what we should pray for as we ought: but the Spirit itself maketh intercession for us with groanings which cannot be uttered.
27 And he that searcheth the hearts knoweth what is the mind of the Spirit, because he maketh intercession for the saints according to the will of God.
28 And we know that all things work together for good to them that love God, to them who are the called according to his purpose.

Praying In The Spirit For Yourself

When I received the mighty baptism with the Holy Spirit, with the initial evidence of speaking with tongues as the Spirit gave utterance (over thirty years ago) it changed my prayer life forever!

While there are many who come against this powerful experience, those who embrace this marvelous grace and gift of God are placed in a glorious position where we can daily commune/communicate with the Father, spirit to Spirit. Speaking with other tongues as the Spirit gives utterance is Spirit talk. It is our spirits being given a language by the Holy Spirit, and being given words from the Holy Spirit which speak to the Father the perfect prayer.

Many come against this kind of prayer because the natural mind does not understand what is being said. However, if we truly believe God, we must trust that His Holy Spirit knows us and knows exactly what we need to pray and what is necessary so that we can comprehend and enter into the perfect plan of the Father – that will and plan which was ordained for our lives from before the very foundation of the world. The Spirit of God knows that plan perfectly. And He knows us perfectly. He knows what words need to be prayed to move us from where we presently are, more and more into the perfect purpose of the Father. We just need to trust Him enough to yield our tongues to Him for a time each day!

Why is this spiritual gift of tongues the very first manifestation that we are given when we are truly baptized with the Holy Spirit? What is it about this gift that causes hell to tremble and religious people to get angry? It is a gifting of the Spirit that literally enables the believer to enter into the realm of God – spirit to Spirit – and speak with the Father in His language and on His level. Yes, we can also do this with the Word, but while our understanding of the Word is limited – very limited – the Holy Spirit knows the perfect will of the Father in full. He, therefore, is able to give us words to pray which transcend our understanding. He gives us the ability to pray for things we do not yet comprehend. As we read in Romans chapter eight, the Spirit comes to our aid and prays for us because we do not know how to pray as we ought. But He does! Now when we read that the Spirit makes intercession for us we must understand that He is not doing this apart from us. No, we must participate in this spiritual process. We have our part to practice. The verse does not say the Holy Spirit will do all of our praying for us. It says He helps us in our weaknesses (infirmities). The Greek word for helps (helpth KJV) here is the word ***synantilambanomai***. According to the **James Strong's Exhaustive Concordance**, it means ***to take hold of opposite together, i.e. co-operate.*** It literally refers to ***taking hold with another against our weaknesses.*** What is one of our weaknesses? We do not know what to pray as we ought. Through the Word we can know what to pray for. However, we do not know what to pray for as we ought. Our understanding of the will, plan and purpose of God is so limited. We have so little understanding of the Word. We need someone to help us pray. We need someone who knows the depths of the Word, who knows the perfect will of God for our lives, who knows exactly what we need to pray and how to offer that prayer in such perfection that the Father hears and responds favorably on our behalf. This is why Jesus sent us the mighty Holy Spirit, bringing with Him that wonderful gift – the prayer language of the Spirit – other tongues. **This is not to take the place of praying the Word.** However, those of us who pray must admit that sometimes we do not know how to pray for things we are facing or things others are facing as we ought. We need help. Until we realize this and understand that this is one of the reasons the Blessed Spirit of God is here – to help us in our prayer life – we shall never be praying all that is necessary for us to enter into the fullness of what has been made ready for us from the foundation of the world. God's will for our lives is perfect. His purpose for our lives is wonderful and fulfilling. Outside of His will, we will never have true satisfaction within. We will always have that awareness that something is missing. We need the Spirit of God. We need His help.

Hell should be afraid! Do you know what it is to be able to pray out the perfect will and purpose of God for your life and for the lives of others in a way that the devil himself is not able to figure out, and therefore, unable to hinder or stop? How can he? He does not even know what you are praying. You may not even know all of what you are praying. At times you can – by the Spirit – pray out in your native tongue what the Spirit gives you in tongues. However, most of the time, you may not know what you are praying, but He does. Wow, oh WOW! I am still amazed at the tremendous love God has for us in giving us such a precious resource and gift. Praying in tongues is a privilege that we should treasure, not fight against.

Praying Through Your Weaknesses

Romans 8:26 (AMPC)
26 So too the [Holy] Spirit comes to our aid and bears us up in our weakness; for we do not know what prayer to offer nor how to offer it worthily as we ought, but the Spirit Himself goes to meet our supplication and pleads in our behalf with unspeakable yearnings and groanings too deep for utterance.

Every believer should meditate upon this scripture often. It holds a major key to victorious kingdom living, for it unveils how the Holy Spirit – the third Member of the Divine God-head – will help us and empower us to get past any lust of the flesh we may be dealing with.

All of us have to deal with the lusts of the flesh, the lusts of the eyes and the pride of life. (See 1John 2:15-17) When the Spirit of God, through the Apostle Paul, spoke of the Holy Spirit helping us in our infirmities, the context of that passage is not referring to sickness or disease. It is referring to weaknesses of the flesh. Whatever lusts or evil desires or passions may be in our flesh, attempting to lure and push us away from the will and ways of God, there is supernatural help – miraculous help – to enable us to walk past it. While the old slogan of "old habits die hard" may be true for those who don't know Christ, the believer has already been made free from sinful habits and lusts. The blood of Christ has made us free. Now, our flesh is not saved yet. It has not yet undergone change. While our inner man – our spirits – have become new creations in Christ Jesus, our bodies (with worldly passions and desires from our past life) are still the same. This is why we must present our bodies to God as living sacrifices. This is why we must change the way we think so that we can make our outward man – our bodies – line up with and transform to what Jesus has done by His Spirit in our inward man. This is why we must practice yielding the members of our bodies to the will and ways of God instead of to sin. (Please Romans 12: 1-2, Romans 6: 11-19 & Romans 8: 1-25)

Now while this may seem like an easy thing, we need help to bring our bodies under subjection. Paul the Apostle spoke of how he had to discipline his flesh.

1Corinthians 9:27
27 But I keep under my body, and bring it into subjection: lest that by any means, when I have preached to others, I myself should be a castaway.

The Amplified Bible Classic Edition says it like this;

1Corinthians 9:27 (AMPC)
27 But [like a boxer] I buffet my body [handle it roughly, discipline it by hardships] and subdue it, for fear that after proclaiming to others the Gospel and things pertaining to it, I myself should become unfit [not stand the test, be unapproved and rejected as a counterfeit].

When writing to the saints at Rome – and to us by extension (for we are all a part of the body of Christ) – Paul, by the Spirit of God, reveals that we need the help of the Holy Spirit to deal with the flesh. The flesh is referring to evil and wrong passions and desires within the body. These, as I said before, most likely developed within us through practice before we received Christ. And since the body has not yet been changed, those desires and passions are still there attempting to find expression. The desire to lie, have sex outside of marriage, hate and be bitter at people, drink what we should not be drinking and the like, have to be mortified. Look at this verse of scripture. We shall look at it in both the King James Version and the Amplified Bible Classic Edition.

Romans 8:13
13 For if ye live after the flesh, ye shall die: but if ye through the Spirit do mortify the deeds of the body, ye shall live.

While we are born again and our spirits have been recreated by the life of God, if we continue following those wrong and sinful passions of lusts that are in our flesh, it will destroy our close intimacy with God, and bring misery and death into our lives. We simply cannot practice the lusts of the flesh and please God. That is not possible. Many sincere believers are battling and struggling in private, not knowing how to put those evil desires to death. Is that even possible? Is it truly possible to literally walk past and live free from those passions which are contrary to the will of God? Yes, it is possible!

Paul says that we can put those ungodly desires to death through the Holy Spirit. He has come to help us. Before we look at the passage in the **Amplified Bible Classic Edition,** let us consider what the word mortify means in this verse. It comes from the **Greek** word *thanatoō*. According to the **James Strong's Exhaustive Concordance,** it means *to (cause to be) put to death or to kill.* So, according to the Word of God, we can put those evil and sinful passions or lusts of our flesh to death. However, we are told that we have to do it through the Spirit. We need His help! Here is the Amplified Bible Classic Edition of that verse.

Romans 8:13 (AMPC)
13 For if you live according to [the dictates of] the flesh, you will surely die. But if through the power of the [Holy] Spirit you are [habitually] putting to death (making extinct, deadening) the [evil] deeds

prompted by the body, you shall [really and genuinely] live forever.

Glory to God Almighty!

It is through the power of the Holy Spirit that we can habitually put the evil deeds prompted by the flesh to death. We can deaden them. We do not have to spend forever fighting the desire to lie, to fornicate, to commit adultery or to steal. We do not have to continually fight malice, unforgiveness, envy or jealousy. We can walk free from these things – one day at a time, one step at a time. How? We need the help of the Holy Spirit. Well, how can we get His help? That is the correct question. He has come to help us pray. Prayer is the key to supernatural empowerment. We need strong spirits. We need a strong inner man to bring that outer man under subjection. This is what the Spirit of God, through the Apostle Paul, was referring to in verses twenty-six through twenty-eight of Romans chapter eight. He says that the Holy Spirit will help us in our infirmities. Remember that the word *"infirmities"* here speaks of those weaknesses of the flesh that we have to deal with. And again, the word *"helpeth"* means that He will take hold together with us against whatever we may be dealing with. How does He do this? He helps us by giving us supernatural groanings which cannot be uttered in our natural language, which includes giving us utterance in other tongues as we yield ourselves to Him in prayer. He gives us His words, His language, His utterance so that we can yield ourselves to Him, praying those words as if it were our prayer – and it is our prayer, inspired of the Holy Spirit. He is the One giving us the words and we are the ones praying them out.

This kind of praying empowers our inner man and infuses us with mighty power so that we can choose to not yield to ungodly desires of the flesh. Instead, we can say no to them, turning our minds and attentions off of those passions and placing them on the will, plan and purpose of the Father. After all, the mind has much to do with the process of mortification. This is why we are instructed to renew our minds.

Our bodies cannot do anything apart from our minds. Our minds are the control center for the body. So, to keep the body under, we must control our thought life. Empowered by the Spirit through prayer, we can do this.

Romans 8: 5 (AMPC)
5 For those who are according to the flesh and are controlled by its unholy desires set their minds on and pursue those things which gratify the flesh, but those who are according to the Spirit and are controlled by the desires of the Spirit set their minds on and seek those things which gratify the [Holy] Spirit.

Consider beloved, the absolute wonder of this majestic offer and opportunity! We have God the Father in Heaven, awaiting our coming to His Throne of mercy and grace. The Lord Jesus Christ – our

Great Intercessor, God the Son – seated at the Father's right hand, awaiting our petitions to present them to the Father on our behalf. And God the Holy Spirit living within us, giving us utterance – the very words to say in prayer – so that we can pray in Heaven's language and receive answers.

Yes, we can and are supposed to pray the Word. But we do not know how to pray as we ought regarding those fleshly lusts that war against our soul. What can we do? Pray in the Spirit. Pray in other tongues. It will build our spirits, empowering us with His strength to deal with those fleshly lusts, giving us the desire and ability to say no to those passions and to walk away from them day by day, step by step. Here is one more verse of scripture to meditate upon in this regard:

1Corinthians 14:4
4 He that speaketh in an unknown tongue edifieth himself; but he that prophesieth edifieth the church.

Take note of the first part of this verse of scripture. When we speak in tongues, we edify ourselves. This is speaking of prayer.

We are building ourselves up. Where is this edification taking place? *It is spiritual edification.* We are building ourselves up in the spirit. Our spirits are being enforced with His mighty power and strength. The word edify is from the **Greek** word *oikodomeō*. The **James Strong Exhaustive**

Specific Kinds Of Prayer

Concordance says it means *to be a house-builder, i.e. construct or (figuratively) confirm.* Through praying in the Spirit, we are literally building ourselves up in our spirits like a builder building an edifice. We are actually improving ourselves spiritually. Do you need improving in your walk with the Lord? I sure do.

Spend some time each day praying in the Holy Spirit. Give yourself to between fifteen minutes or more daily giving the Holy Spirit the opportunity to help you in your prayer life. He will empower your inner man. He will strengthen you on the inside. He will give your inward man power to rise up and tell the flesh no when it may want to misbehave. If your flesh has been giving you issues, spend time in the Word of God daily and spend time praying in the Spirit. The more time we give to prayer in the spirit, the more change takes place within us. Be diligent to do this consistently. We are not helpless. We have help. We have the Helper!

Jude 20 (AMPC)
20 But you, beloved, build yourselves up [founded] on your most holy faith [make progress, rise like an edifice higher and higher], praying in the Holy Spirit;

Let us now consider praying in the Spirit for others.

Work Sheet

What is praying in the Spirit? Two answers required.
_____
_____
_____

Why is praying in the Spirit so important to the believer?
_____
_____
_____

How does the Holy Spirit help us in our prayer life?
_____
_____
_____
_____

How does the Holy Spirit help us to mortify the evil deeds of the flesh?
_____
_____
_____
_____

Specific Kinds Of Prayer

Chapter Twelve
IN THE SPIRIT FOR OTHERS

Ephesians 6:18 (AMPC)
18 Pray at all times (on every occasion, in every season) in the Spirit, with all [manner of] prayer and entreaty. To that end keep alert and watch with strong purpose and perseverance, interceding in behalf of all the saints (God's consecrated people).

What a wonderful, joyous and marvelous experience to be able to communicate with the Father God, spirit to Spirit. When we pray in other tongues, it is our spirits speaking to God the Father of spirits, by the Holy Spirit. We are encouraged to pray in the Spirit and in our natural language.

1Corinthians 14:14-15 (AMPC)
14 For if I pray in an [unknown] tongue, my spirit [by the Holy Spirit within me] prays, but my mind

is unproductive [it bears no fruit and helps nobody].
15 Then what am I to do? I will pray with my spirit [by the Holy Spirit that is within me], but I will also pray [intelligently] with my mind and understanding; I will sing with my spirit [by the Holy Spirit that is within me], but I will sing [intelligently] with my mind and understanding also.

When we pray in the Spirit, it is the Holy Spirit giving our spirits the utterance or language, and we are therefore praying by His wisdom and guidance. Prayer in this way is limitless, for the Spirit of God knows all things. He knows what is going on with everyone everywhere. He, therefore, knows what needs to be prayed so that the will and purpose of the Father can be done. While this is for our personal benefit, praying in the Spirit will also benefit others that we pray for as well.

Our prayers for the saints should be done in the natural and in the Spirit, for the Spirit of God knows what is going one with each believer and with every single person on the face of this planet. Paul, by the Spirit of God, encourages us to pray at all times in the Spirit. Of course, this means praying by the leadership of the Spirit or as one is led by the Spirit, but it also refers to praying in the Spirit – in other tongues. This is where He is able to give us the exact words to say in prayer, where we are praying beyond our intellect and what we limitedly comprehend. We are praying the very Mind of Christ for whoever we are praying for. The Spirit of the Living God is giving us what needs to be prayed.

It is always worthwhile, when praying for others, to pray with what understanding we do have, according to the Word of God in Jesus Name, and then to spend some time praying in the Holy Spirit. Whatever we may be missing, He will address as we yield our tongues to Him.

Look once again at what God says in Romans chapter eight.

Romans 8: 26-27
26 Likewise the Spirit also helpeth our infirmities: for we know not what we should pray for as we ought: but the Spirit itself maketh intercession for us with groanings which cannot be uttered.
27 And he that searcheth the hearts knoweth what is the mind of the Spirit, because he maketh intercession for the saints according to the will of God.

We do not know what to pray for as we ought. This would definitely include our prayers for fellow believers!

A lot of times, we sense that our prayers for others seem so inadequate. They may be facing some spiritual battle. They may be in the midst of a severe test or trial. Perhaps they may have some tragedy or be hurting because of issues in their family life. Yes, sometimes they may be dealing with a sickness or

Specific Kinds Of Prayer

disease where they may die if God does not intervene. Here is an example of how I pray for others:

Father, in the Name of the Lord Jesus, I come to You today, giving You thanks and praise for Your lovingkindness and Your tender mercies. I come on behalf of _____ who stands in needs of prayer. Father, _____ is in need of_____. They need Your help. I am coming because, according to Your Word, You said _____ (Based upon the need, I will bring the Father's Word to Him. This is covenant talk). Father, intervene on _____ behalf.

Touch _____ right now. Heal right now. Minister to them right now. (Then I will say), Dear Holy Spirit. I have prayed with what limited understanding I have regarding this situation. I am leaning upon You Sir, asking for You to give me utterance so that I can pray according to the perfect will of God for _____ in Jesus Name. You know exactly what they need and so I yield my tongue to You that I may pray for them in Jesus Name.

Then I will begin praying in tongues, in the Spirit, totally depending upon the Holy Spirit to pray the will of the Father for whomever I am praying for. Most of the time, while I am praying in tongues, at some point I sense the Spirit of God coming upon me stronger and stronger, and the utterance of the Spirit seems to get stronger and stronger. I pray in this manner until I can sense that I have prayed the matter through and I sense a release of the Spirit. Sometimes I laugh in the Spirit. At other times, I sense that I have prayed it through and have a *'Divine assurance'* that it is done. I will give the Father thanks and praise for hearing my prayer in Jesus Name. By the way, when praying for the lost, I pray a very similar prayer. I bind the devil from the person in Jesus Name, claiming his or her full salvation and deliverance in Jesus Name. I ask God to send forth laborers – the right person or persons that the individual would listen to – across their path. Then I would begin praying in tongues, believing for the Holy Spirit to give me utterance so that I pray according to the perfect will of the Father for that individual. Of course, that person has a will. My prayer is not to override their will. Rather, God, through prayer, will do whatever He needs to do to ensure they have all the opportunity necessary to respond to the Gospel.

Praying in the Spirit is powerful. Paul the Apostle said these words regarding his prayer life. He apparently spoke in tongues continually. He understood the value of doing so. May we follow in his footsteps that we may enjoy the benefits of praying in the Spirit as well! Here is what he said.

1Corinthians 14:18
18 I thank my God, I speak with tongues more than ye all.

Now let us look at how the **Amplified Bible Classic Edition** translates this verse. It is enlightening and gives us a glimpse into the tremendous place Paul's gave to praying in other tongues.

1Corinthians 14:18 (AMPC)
18 I thank God that I speak in [strange] tongues (languages) more than any of you or all of you put together;

Obviously, he prayed much in the Spirit. He said that he did more than all of those believers who were at Corinth, all of them put together. This means that he gave much value to this kind of praying. We should follow his example.

After over thirty years of being filled with God's Holy Spirit, and praying much in other tongues, I also say, *"I thank my God I speak with tongues."*

Specific Kinds Of Prayer

Work Sheet

What are our infirmities in regard to prayer?
_____
_____
_____

How are we to pray for fellow-believers?
_____
_____
_____
_____
_____

How can we pray for other believers when we do not know exactly what to pray for?
_____
_____
_____

When we pray in other tongues, what are we doing? Multiple answers.
_____
_____
_____
_____
_____
_____
_____

Specific Kinds Of Prayer

Chapter Thirteen
DEVELOPING A PRAYER LIFE

Prayer is personal and corporate!

Developing a life of prayer is the result of daily practice. Every one of us should enter into intimacy with the Father in this manner. After all, He paid an awesome price so that we could come into His presence and fellowship with Him.

What was the purpose of the cross? It was so that we could know Him. It was so that each of us could become His children and experience and enjoy real closeness with Him. We can be as close to Him as we choose to be. This is not reserved for just some apostle or some prophet, some pope or some priest. All of us can have – and enjoy – intimacy with our Father through prayer. He loves us. He truly does!

Look at this verse of scripture. Look at why Jesus died for us God wanted us. Oh, how He loves us:

1Corinthian 2:6 (AMPC)
7 But rather what we are setting forth is a wisdom of God once hidden [from the human understanding] and now revealed to us by God—[that wisdom] which God devised and decreed before the ages for our glorification [to lift us into the glory of His presence].

This was the reason for Calvary. God wants us to live in His Presence. We do this through prayer!

Prayer is the place of power with God. It is vital that we pray daily. We are admonished to pray without ceasing. (See 1Thessalonians 5:17) This means that we are to develop the habit of seeking the Face of God, that we practice acknowledging Him in all of our ways, so that He can direct our paths. It describes the blessedness of being ever mindful of His Presence within us, and practicing His Presence by learning to speak with Him, consult with Him, listen for Him and obey Him. The more we spend time in His Word and developing a life of prayer, the closer we will draw to Him. He promised that as we draw nearer to Him, He would draw nearer to us. Yes, He lives within us, but we will come to experience His closeness in ways that are truly intimate and life-transforming. Prayer is a part of the process of drawing near. (Read Proverbs 3: 5-6 & James 4:8)

Those who practice His Presence by developing closeness with Him through earnest, sincere, genuine, heart-felt prayer enter into places of His glory that are easily discerned. As a matter of fact, there are those who carry the sense of His Presence in and around them in such a manner that one can sense (feel) His Presence when that person enters a room. His Glory upon a believer can become so strong that the moment he or she begins to pray in public, God's Presence permeates the atmosphere. Some carry such an aroma of His Presence that it makes the lukewarm believer miserable, the religious person nervous or angry, and bring sinners under conviction without a word being spoken about God. Yes, this is very possible. God's Presence becomes tangible in the life of the person who practices His Presence in prayer.

The Purpose Of The Cross

The prayer-less believer is a powerless believer. The prayer-less church is a powerless church. However, when an individual believer or a local assembly is given to prayer, the Spirit of God is always active within that life or that assembly!

When our Lord went to the cross as the Lamb of God for our sins, something happened which should excite the heart of every believer. Here is what the Word says.

Matthew 27:51
51 And, behold, the veil of the temple was rent in twain from the top to the bottom; and the earth did quake, and the rocks rent;

This is marvelous and reveals God's great love for each of us!

The torn veil is powerful for it reveals God's invitation to each and every person on the face of this planet to draw near to Him and to know Him for oneself. To understand it, we shall have to consider the Tabernacle of Moses that God told him to make. It was a shadow and type of the reality which we now have in Jesus Christ. The Bible says, **"The law was given by Moses, but grace and truth (reality) came by Jesus Christ."** (See John 1:17)

When God told Moses to build the tabernacle, He gave him the blueprint and Moses built it as instructed. The tabernacle had an outer court, the holy place and the most holy place. In the holy place was the table of showbread, which represents continual feeding upon the precious Word of God; and the golden candlestick, which represents the working of the Holy Spirit within the believer's soul. Then as one proceeded to enter the most holy place, there was an altar – the altar of incense – which represents the place of prayer and worship of the believer. Then there was a veil which separated the holy place from the most holy place. Only the high priest had the permission of the Most High God to enter into the very holy of holies where the Presence of God would be. No one else could enter. To attempt to do so would result in death. The Bible teaches that this was because *the way* into the holiest of all had not yet been made. We italicized those words – *the way* – because *the way* is a Person. (Read Hebrews 9

& John 14:6) So, under the Old Covenant, only the high priest could enter into His glorious Presence within the veil. He went in alone to pray for the sins of the people and for his own sins. The same held true in the Temple of Solomon. It held true until that day when **'The Way of God'** went to the cross in a physical body as our substitute and as the Lamb of God – shedding His precious and holy blood for our sins. The veil of the temple there in Jerusalem was torn in two by an unseen power. God was showing these two powerful realities:

1. *That God would no longer live in that temple, but would now come to live within the hearts of all who receive Jesus Christ as Lord and Savior. (Think about that. We are God indwelt).*

2. *That God, through His Son, "The WAY," opened the way into His Presence for all who truly desire to be His and to know Him. We can all come into His very Presence for ourselves. We can do so whenever we want and as often as we would like. As a matter of fact, His invitation is that we live in His Presence by praying without ceasing. We can be as close to Father God as we choose to!*

Armed with this information, what are you prepared to do?

Will you stay on the outside, living a lukewarm life of prayerlessness and powerlessness? Will you just depend on others to draw near to God for you while you waste all of your time on things which simply do not matter? Will you allow social media and the like to continually consume your time, neglecting His glorious standing invitation for ***"whosoever will?"*** Or will you make it your business to draw nearer and nearer to God the Father, in the Name of Jesus, by the Holy Spirit through developing a life-style of prayer?

He longs for you to know Him. He paid the price of blood to make it possible. Now it is up to each of us to show Him how much we truly appreciate what He has done for and in us by giving ourselves to seeking His Face in prayer.

May this short guide on prayer assist you in developing your prayer life, experiencing and enjoying the true wonders of His Person and the glory of His Presence!

Work Sheet

What is the true purpose of prayer?
_____
_____
_____

How can we practice the Presence of God on an ongoing basis?
_____
_____
_____

What does it mean to pray without ceasing?
_____
_____
_____

What 3 things can one do daily which leads to closeness with the Lord?
_____
_____
_____

What was the main lessons you learned from this book?
_____
_____
_____

THE PRAYER OF SALVATION

The Most Important Prayer You Will Ever Pray

Dear friend, are you ready to be a part of the family of God and enjoy the awesome and abundant life that God desires for you?

He loves you so much and wants you so much. He knew you could not come to Him on your own and with your good works. They could never qualify you to stand in His presence for you were born in sin and shaped in iniquity. The Great and Loving God, seeing your dilemma sent His Son, the Lord Jesus Christ to pay the price of your sins with His blood; His holy and precious blood to redeem you to Himself and through that redemption, bring you into a relationship with Him.

John 3:16 says,
"For God so loved the world, that He gave His only begotten Son, that whosoever believeth in Him, should not perish, but have everlasting life."

Jesus Christ, God's Son is the only way to God the Father (John 14:6). Through His death, burial, and resurrection, He provided salvation from sin and newness of life. To receive God's gift of eternal life and become a part of His family, please pray this prayer and mean it with all your heart:

Oh God in heaven, I come to you in the name of your Son, the Lord Jesus Christ. Your Word declares that the person who comes to you, you will not cast away (John 6:37). So I know that you receive me now. I believe Jesus died for me and shed His precious and holy blood to wash away my sins. I believe that You raised Him from the dead. Right now, I receive Jesus Christ as my Lord and personal Savior. Jesus is my Lord.
Father, You said in Your Word that if I do this I would be saved (Romans 10:9-10). So I now confess and boldly declare, according to God's Word, I am saved. I am born again. I am a child of God (John 1:12).
Thank You Father for receiving me, saving me, and making me a new creation in Christ Jesus (2 Corinthians 5:17).
Fill me with Your precious Holy Spirit and empower and help me to live this life for You. In Jesus Name I pray, amen.

If you prayed to receive Christ as your Lord and personal Savior, please email me and let me know. I would love to hear from you. My email address is: *sheldond.newton@gmail.com*

Specific Kinds Of Prayer

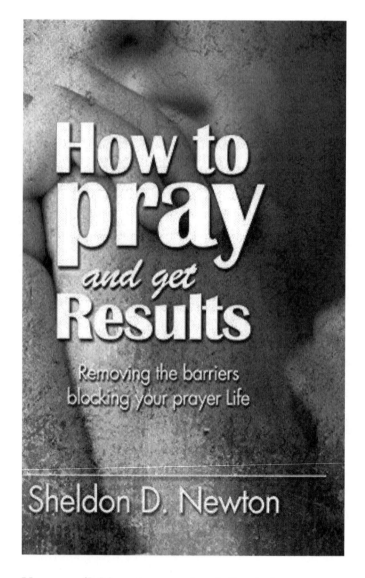

Now available at your local bookstore or on amazon.com

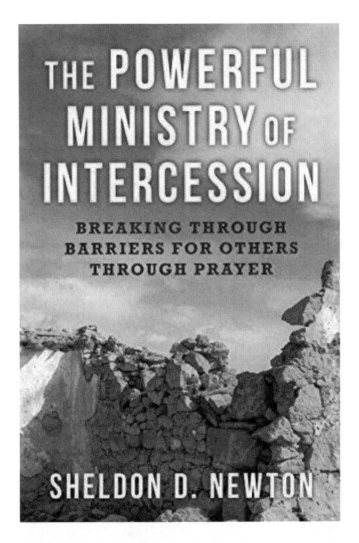

Available at your local bookstore or on amazon.com

Now available at your local bookstore or on amazon.com

Now available in your local bookstore or on amazon.com

Now available at your local bookstore.

Now available at your local bookstore.

Now available at your local bookstore.

CONTACT INFORMATION

For prayer, or to contact Dr. Newton for speaking engagements, please email him at:

sheldond.newton@gmail.com

Or visit our website at

www.sheldondnewton.org

You can mail Dr. Newton at:

Dr. Sheldon D. Newton
P. O. Box N. 10257
Nassau, Bahamas

Specific Kinds Of Prayer

Made in the USA
Middletown, DE
19 November 2024

64958094R00097